TEN GUIDELINES TO HELP YOU ACHIEVE YOUR LONG-AWAITED

PROMOTION!

POWERFUL PRINCIPLES TO HELP DETERMINE IF YOU OR SOMEONE ELSE IS READY TO BE PROMOTED INTO NEW REALMS OF AUTHORITY AND RESPONSIBILITY

RICK RENNER

TEACH ALL NATIONS

A book company anointed to take God's Word
to you and to the nations of the world.

a division of
RICK RENNER MINISTRIES

This book is *fabulous*! Rick reminds you that to be a leader, you don't have to be perfect, but you must be willing to grow and to keep on growing! If you are already in leadership, Rick teaches you how to mentor promising leaders so they become top-notch producers who please God. This book is a real teaching tool you have to read to appreciate. If you read it, you'll grow as I have.

— *Dexter Yager*
Quixtar's Network Marketing Genius

This book is a "must-read" for anyone in leadership or desiring to be promoted into a leadership position. The principles Rick Renner shares apply to both ministries and business organizations of all types whose leaders desire to fulfill God's purpose in their endeavors. Reading this book has prompted me to reexamine my own organizational structure. I wish my grandfather (Armand Hammer) was alive to see the impact that Rick is making in Russia!

— *Michael Armand Hammer*
Chairman and CEO of
The Armand Hammer Foundation

From Rick's incredible life, he realistically and profoundly shares ten keys every leader must apply to be successful and to build a great team. If you're looking for the same old milk, skip this book. But if you want something really meaty — something that really works — this is the book you've been looking for!

— *John Mason*
Best-selling author of
An Enemy Called Average

This is a power-packed book, loaded with vital principles and practical insights for growing a successful business and for choosing leaders who will help you realize your goals and dreams. We've implemented these principles ourselves, and God's blessing on our business has been the result!

— Wallace and June Blume
Owners, Denali Flavors, Inc.
("Moose Tracks" Ice Cream)

This book is jam-packed with practical wisdom and rich spiritual insights that are great for those who desire to excel in life. Pastors will want every member of their churches to read this book — and I can't think of a better resource to use as part of a curriculum to provide ongoing training to staff, leaders, and workers.

— Tony Cooke
President, Tony Cooke Ministries

Dr. Renner outlines for us the requirements for genuine promotion with time-proven principles that, when acted upon and executed, will help any leader choose qualified leaders and build an unbeatable team. This book will help anyone who desires to go beyond vision and into action.

— Dr. Robert Daniels Thompson
Vice Chairman, The Gabriel Call
President, International College of Excellence

Ten Guidelines To Help You Achieve Your Long-Awaited Promotion!
ISBN-13: 978-0-9725454-6-4
ISBN-10: 0-9725454-6-8
Previously entitled *Who Is Ready for a Spiritual Promotion?*
Copyright © 2000 by Rick Renner
P. O. Box 702040
Tulsa, OK 74170-2040

Revised Edition 2005
2nd Printing

Editorial Consultant: Cynthia Hansen
Text Design: Lisa Simpson

DEDICATION

It is with great joy that I dedicate this book to all the team members whom God has called to work alongside Denise and me as we give our all to fulfill God's call on our lives. Denise and I may be the leaders and the faces that are most visible, but we are well aware that much of what has been accomplished is due to the grace of God and to colaborers who have been willing to do whatever is required to accomplish the job God has entrusted into our hands.

Thank you for your courage, your commitment, and your boldness to follow the Holy Spirit and to submit to my spiritual authority and leadership. We are blessed that you have been a part of our lives, and Denise and I love you more than we'll ever know how to express. We are so grateful for your partnership in the Gospel of the Lord Jesus Christ.

CONTENTS

FOREWORD

It has been my privilege to serve at Rick Renner's side since 1991. First, I came to know Rick as one of his Bible school students. After graduation, I became Rick's interpreter. Then I became his coworker in developing and establishing the *Good News Television Network*. Today I serve as Rick's associate in *Rick Renner Ministries*, in the *Good News Church*, and in the *Good News Association of Pastors and Churches*.

Through all these years of working with Rick, he has become not only my boss but also my dearest friend. He is the most influential leader in my life, helping to bring me to a higher level of excellence in my life and ministry. He has also cultivated in me the strategic leadership skills I need to do what God has called me to do.

In this book, Rick outlines his practical approach to leadership selection. As I have worked closely with him from day to day, I have seen in action the principles he has written in this book in many different situations. I can testify from firsthand experience that they work, because I have seen the fruit produced by them.

I wholeheartedly recommend this book to every person who is in leadership and to those who long to be leaders. Anyone who carefully and prayerfully applies these principles will see for himself that they work!

I'm excited for you to have this book. I believe it will be a blessing to you, just as the truths contained in its pages have been and continue to be a blessing to me.

Andrey Chebotarev
Ministry Associate
Rick Renner Ministries
and Good News Church
March, 2000

INTRODUCTION

As I fulfill the call on my life to work with local churches all over the former Soviet Union, I find myself constantly assisting pastors who have serious problems with their leaders or staff members. When I ask how these problematic leaders were first chosen for leadership, I find they were frequently chosen too fast and without proper testing to see what kind of leaders they would be and how they would perform in different situations.

The church is growing so rapidly in this region of the world that there is a great shortage of leaders. In fact, pastors have been so desperate for leaders to help them in their growing churches that they've unintentionally ignored Paul's command in First Timothy 5:22 to "lay hands suddenly on no man...."

As a result, pastors are sometimes caught in a conflict with leaders who *never* should have been placed in a leadership position. These pastors start "back-peddling," trying to figure out how to get certain people *out of* leadership who should have never been placed *into* leadership. This difficult situation was created when new people were made a part of the team before those in charge really knew them.

I have written this book to help pastors and leaders of ministries make right choices when choosing members of their team. The principles found in this book are the same ones I have followed in my own ministry. Certainly these principles are neither perfect nor complete in their presentation. However, the ten basic points that follow have served as effective guidelines to help me and my team make sound leadership choices through the years.

In this book, I share both our mistakes and our victories. I also share what we've learned from our mistakes and how the Lord has taught us to move carefully and more accurately when choosing key members for the inner circle of our team.

Although the principles found in this book are written with churches and ministries in mind, they can be applied to any kind of business or organization as well. Also, these guidelines are not based on local cultural situations but on principles from God's Word. Therefore, they may serve as cross-cultural guidelines, applicable to churches, ministries, businesses, or organizations in any region of the world.

I trust this book will help you make sound choices as you build your own team for your God-given assignment and territory in the Kingdom of God.

Rick Renner
March, 2000

THE ACID TEST
FOR LEADERSHIP

*H*aving been tested over the years *by* leadership before I was allowed *to be* a leader, I can personally vouch for the benefits of this experience. It didn't make me worse; it made me *better*. In fact, it saved me from a lot of trouble I would have experienced later on in life.

Now as a leader, I am in a position where I must discern if God-called people are ready at any given moment to assume new levels of responsibility. I value the process of testing people *before* I allow them to serve in any leadership capacity with me. A part of me feels compassion for those being tested. But on the other hand, I'm thrilled they have the opportunity to be changed by the same fire that changed and delivered me from so much that needed to be removed from my life.

You see, tests are just a part of life. Whether or not we face these tests willingly is up to us. Nevertheless, it's a fact that we will all be tested at different times in our lives.

These tests often arise in the interplay of relationships. You see, although relationships are precious gifts from God, every relationship is tested at some point. For instance, when people begin to "rub shoulder to shoulder," working together in a close environment, sparks of strife can sometimes ignite when wills or personalities collide or when people hold different opinions about a particular subject or direction to be taken. These collision points frequently reveal whether or not people possess the compatibility to work together on one team.

> Although relationships are precious gifts from God, every relationship is tested at some point.

So before you invest yourself into a new follower or give yourself fully to a new leader, first make sure you and he are compatible. It's a waste of valuable time, effort, and energy to invest massive amounts of time and energy into a person and then afterward decide he isn't a right fit.

It's better to commit yourself to a prospective leader with both eyes wide open, knowing exactly what you're doing and exactly what you're getting. If you enter that relationship blindly, you'll later regret that you didn't take more time before you sealed the deal.

Once you've taken the time and the right measures to confirm that God is leading you to enter this relationship, go full-steam ahead, holding nothing back. Be committed to forge through any obstacle that may try to block your path.

Even if you run into a conflict of will, personality, or philosophy with that person, don't give up on the relationship as long as you *know* the Lord put you in it. Don't let anyone or any kind of friction drive you out of that commitment.

Jesus said, "...Let your 'Yes' be 'Yes,' and your 'No,' 'No'..." (Matthew 5:37 *NIV*). If you sense the Lord telling you, "Yes, you are to work with this person," you must stick with what He has put in your heart!

You see, God isn't like some people who are constantly changing their mind, telling you one thing one day and a different thing the next day (Numbers 23:19). If today He tells you to enter into a working relationship with a person, He isn't going to tell you tomorrow, "Oops! I made a mistake! I was wrong — I really don't want you to work with this person after all!"

> If you sense the Lord telling you, "Yes, you are to work with this person," you must stick with what He has put in your heart!

This is why you must move slowly and be absolutely sure you are hearing God correctly before choosing someone for your leadership team.

> Move slowly and be absolutely sure you are hearing God correctly before choosing someone for your leadership team.

Once you know that God is telling you to join yourself to a person, go forward as though you are specially commissioned by God to do it. There will always be moments that arise to make you question your decision, so it's important that you nail it down and make absolutely sure you're standing on solid ground when you publicly announce your decision to work alongside this person.

TEN GUIDELINES TO DETERMINE IF A PERSON IS COMPATIBLE WITH YOU

In the following chapters, I want to give you ten guidelines I've used in my own ministry to determine if a person is compatible to work on my leadership team. These practical, down-to-earth suggestions are intended to test a prospective candidate and reveal if he has the right kind of heart for holding a leadership position in a church, ministry, business, or organization. When these suggestions are followed, they nearly always expose any problems a leader needs to know *before* he gives a person a place at his side.

The truth is, people who serve with us *will* be tested, whether we test them deliberately or not. As I said, every relationship is tested at some point. So the purpose of these ten guidelines is not to teach leaders how to put prospective leaders through a grueling ordeal. Rather, my desire is to equip leaders with the ability to enter into each new working relationship with eyes wide open so they won't later be shocked or disappointed with the person they have chosen for a leadership position.

I've also found that as the testing process progresses, not only do the leaders learn about the newcomers, but the newcomers learn a lot about those whom they're going to follow and serve. This kind of insight may seem difficult to receive at first, but ultimately it helps the newcomer become a better leader.

You see, often people become enamored with a spiritual leader and fantasize about what it must be like to work alongside that person. But once their dream comes true and their job begins, they discover their leader is still very much a human with clay feet!

When the preconceived illusion these followers possessed dissipates and fades in the true light of the spiritual leader's humanity, they often are left feeling let down and disappointed. But the expectations they held concerning that leader were *unrealistic.*

UNREALISTIC EXPECTATIONS OF LEADERS BRING ONLY DISAPPOINTMENT

I remember an event in my own life many years ago that illustrates this point.

I deeply loved and respected the pastor who first hired me as a full-time associate minister. He treated me like a son and began to teach me the "ins and outs" of ministry. He knew Greek; he was a respected scholar; and he had a library of more than twenty thousand books — all of which he had read! He taught like a university professor, and he loved his people. He was the personification of everything I dreamed for my own life.

A rarity in his denomination, this pastor truly embraced the gifts of the Holy Spirit and allowed them to operate in the context of his church. He possessed a beautiful, balanced mix of intellectualism and spirituality that I had rarely seen in a pastor.

I was a young man just starting in the ministry, but this godly minister showed me a great deal of attention, helping to build my self-confidence. It was simply amazing that a man of this caliber would devote so much of himself to a man as young as I was at that time. He loved me, believed in me, and invested himself in me.

This pastor taught me how to use my knowledge of the Greek language with integrity, and he showed me how to exercise wisdom in the way I taught the Word. He lovingly instructed me in the practical aspects of the ministry, including scheduling, finances, counseling, and even how to conduct myself with people in difficult situations. And when it was necessary, he rebuked me and brought correction to areas of my life that needed attention.

I loved this man and listened carefully to the instructions he gave me each day. In my sight, he could do nothing wrong. *My appraisal of him was so high, I was inevitably destined to be disappointed somewhere along the way.* I didn't realize what I was doing at the time, but I had placed this man on a dangerously high pedestal. In my mind, he was nearly equal to the apostle Paul.

As we worked more and more closely together, I began to see normal human frailties in this pastor that wouldn't have upset or disappointed me in anyone else. But I didn't want to believe he was like anyone else. So when I saw him do things that were just a shade lower than my expectations, it threw me into a maze of confusion and bewilderment. If he did something that seemed inconsistent or ugly, I'd try to dismiss it as my imagination. I had an illusion of this man that was totally unrealistic and that neither he nor anyone else could have ever lived up to.

I'll never forget the day I realized this pastor wasn't perfect. Waves of disappointment washed over my emotions. My idol was shattered. As I judged him for failing my illusion of the person I thought he was, I completely forgot that I was guilty of the same mistakes for which I was judging him. I had placed expectations on him that I didn't even demand or expect of myself! It wasn't realistic and it wasn't fair. *I expected him to be super-human — and no one is super-human.*

I learned a difficult lesson at that early stage of my ministry when I came to terms with my pastor's normal humanity and accepted the fact he wasn't perfect. But I thank God for this experience. Now that I'm a spiritual leader myself, I have special mercy for those who work close to me. I know how easy it would be for them to make the same mistake I did years ago by placing unrealistic expectations on *me.*

Today when someone comes to work in our ministry, I warn them that I am a completely normal human being who needs to have his mind renewed and who is growing in Jesus just like everyone else. Yes, I'm a leader who should be respected and honored, but I don't want them to have illusions about me that I'll never be able to live up to.

I've personally found it better to tell my team members the truth about myself from the start than to let them go through the horrible disillusionment process I went through so many years ago. It's not that I'm so terrible. But I am a normal person, and I don't want people to become disappointed when they see me act like a human being from time to time.

Flesh is flesh, and as long as believers live in their earthen vessels, they will have to deal with issues of the flesh in their lives. Even those who seem to be the most spiritually mature must deal with their flesh, just like everyone else.

ALL LEADERS HAVE HUMAN FRAILTIES

Psalm 103:13,14 says, "Like as a father pitieth his children, so the Lord pitieth them that fear him. For he knoweth our frame; he remembereth that we are dust." God knows that even the most committed of His children are made of dust.

God does put a lot of expectations on us, but He knows it's difficult to expect perfection from dust! I cling to this verse when I know I've come short of what I need to be.

In moments when I'm tempted to judge myself too sternly for being human, I remind myself, *Rick, God remembers that you're made of dust. Do the best you can, but don't get upset if you're not 100% accurate all the time. Your spirit may be newly created in Christ Jesus, but you're still living in a body that's made out of dust. You should do the best you can at everything you do, but you cannot expect perfection from dust!*

As we look at both the Old and New Testament, we can see that all of God's leaders were flawed in some way. Just consider these examples:

Abraham made almost comical mistakes as he started his walk of faith. In fact, if a modern-day believer made the mistakes today that Abraham did centuries ago, the believer probably wouldn't even be considered for leadership in his church! Yet God called Abraham *the father of faith*!

How about Moses?

Moses was so temperamental that when he struck the rock with the rod in his hand and the water didn't come out as quickly as he wanted, he struck it a second time in anger!

24

Because of that moment of rage, God forbade him to enter the Promised Land (Numbers 20:10-12). Moses had a temper! Yet he was one of God's most anointed leaders.

How about David?

Rather than fight on the field with his men, David stayed home and committed adultery with Bathsheba. Then he deliberately sent her husband Uriah to the frontlines of battle to be killed so he could marry Bathsheba (2 Samuel 11). Even though these inconsistencies are totally unacceptable for a man of God, this is the same person the Bible called "a man after God's own heart" (1 Samuel 13:14)! In fact, it was through David's lineage that Jesus was born!

How about Elijah?

This mighty prophet of God fearlessly challenged the prophets of Baal one day — and then ran away in fright from Queen Jezebel the next day when she threatened his life (1 Kings 18:17-40; 19:1-4). What do you suppose Elijah's actions looked like to those who knew he had called fire down from heaven and then slain 450 prophets of Baal with the sword just one day earlier? No doubt the prophet Elijah seemed a little inconsistent!

After he had run from Jezebel for an entire day, this same mighty prophet found himself sitting under a juniper tree in the wilderness, wailing and feeling sorry for himself — *all because a woman was mad at him!* This definitely wasn't behavior befitting a man who had called fire down from heaven and killed 450 prophets of Baal the day before!

How about the apostle Peter?

Peter was always trying to be the leader of the group. He was also constantly speaking out of turn and putting his foot in his mouth by saying stupid things that he probably later regretted.

On the night Jesus was betrayed, Peter was the one who rose up like a mercenary soldier in the Garden of Gethsemane. Reaching for a sword, he bravely assaulted Malchus, the servant of the high priest, cutting off the servant's ear as he attempted to defend Jesus (John 18:10).

Do you think Peter was *aiming for the servant's ear?* Why would anyone attack an ear? I've never heard of anyone trying to cut off someone's ear, have you? I believe Peter was aiming for the man's head and missed, swiping the man's ear by mistake. But Jesus just touched the servant, and he was healed (Luke 22:51).

What did Jesus think about Peter's actions that night? Jesus knew it was His time to be arrested and crucified. He was ready for God's plan to be activated; He knew He had to be offered as the spotless Lamb for the sin of the world. Jesus had no intentions of resisting.

Suddenly Peter jumped in the middle of God's business and tried to create a revolt. So even as Jesus faced His arrest and the prospect of an illegal trial, a vicious scourging, and the cruelty of crucifixion, He had to stop and clean up the mess Peter created in the Garden of Gethsemane. Jesus took the time to heal Malchus' ear, perhaps because He didn't want Peter to be arrested for his impulsive actions.

But then look at what happened to this same Peter who seemed so brave in the Garden of Gethsemane. Later that same night, Peter denied that he even knew Jesus *three separate times* (John 18:15-18, 25-27). Talk about *inconsistency*!

How about Paul and Barnabas?

These two mighty New Testament leaders disputed about whether or not they should take John Mark on their next journey. Paul and Barnabus got so upset with each other that they nearly slugged it out right in front of the whole church (Acts 15:37-39). Does this seem like correct behavior for the man God used to write the majority of the New Testament epistles? No, but it demonstrates the fact that even Paul wasn't perfect!

I know many well-known spiritual leaders who are alive today. *They are my personal friends.* I could use some of them as modern-day examples of how God uses normal, common, flawed human beings. But rather than go into detail about them, let me assure you that God is still in the business of using people made of dust (Psalm 103:14).

Perhaps no illustration of this truth is clearer to me personally than the fact that God has chosen to use *me.* I am amazed that God has chosen me because I know *me so* well. I know my flesh, my struggles, my inconsistencies, and the weak areas of my life that I'm endeavoring to conquer and bring up to a higher level.

Like all of God's leaders, I have areas where I need to change and grow. I don't want anyone to hold on to a preconceived, unrealistic illusion that I'm a perfect leader.

If a newcomer to our team has the false illusion that I walk on clouds 99% of the time, he or she is going to be sorely disappointed. I'm a normal man, called by God, walking by faith, just like everyone else. I'm learning to bring my flesh into subjection so God can use me in a greater way, just like everyone else. I'm constantly growing, but I'm certainly not where I want to be yet.

Unrealistic Expectations of Followers Also Cause Disappointment

Sometimes leaders make this same mistake by having unrealistically high expectations of their followers. Perhaps a leader observes someone in his church, ministry, or business whom he believes has incredible potential to do something great. As a result, the leader may unintentionally form an unrealistic opinion about that person that produces a false illusion. Often this preconceived opinion is so exaggerated that the person could never live up to the leader's expectations.

I've made this mistake on several occasions. You see, I believe in people and in their ability to do something great with their lives. But several times I've made the mistake of believing a person had greater abilities than he really possessed. Perhaps his potential was truly phenomenal. However, because of his lack of experience or self-confidence, that person wasn't able to do what I had hoped he could do.

I've had to learn to refrain from placing unrealistic expectations upon people. Yes, I expect them to do their best, but I *don't* expect them to live up to an unrealistic idea of what I hope they can be. That isn't fair to them, and it results in disappointment for me.

In the end, any leader becomes disappointed and feels let down when he discovers that a promising follower isn't as perfect as he had expected. That's why leaders must come to understand that just as *they* are "made of dust," any person they choose to work alongside of them is made of dust as well. Therefore, the same grace and mercy the leader expects others to offer him, he must also extend to the follower he has chosen to be a part of his team.

No person chosen to work on your leadership team will always do everything perfectly. There will be moments of misunderstanding, differences of opinion, and other unpredictable factors. At times, team members will even hold contrary views to what you hold to be true. But this is all part of the package you have to accept when you work with human beings.

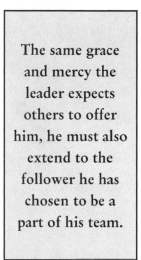

The same grace and mercy the leader expects others to offer him, he must also extend to the follower he has chosen to be a part of his team.

When you select people to become part of your leadership team, you have to recognize their strengths without forgetting that you'll be surprised by their weaknesses along the way as well. But don't feel let down or discouraged when you run into one of those weaknesses. Remember, your team members have probably encountered a few surprises in *your* personality too!

It's good to believe in people and to expect them to perform at the highest level they're capable of. This is especially true of

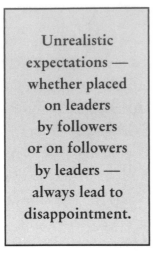

Unrealistic
expectations —
whether placed
on leaders
by followers
or on followers
by leaders —
always lead to
disappointment.

Christians, for everything believers do should be done "as unto the Lord," carried out to the best of their ability (Ephesians 6:7; Colossians 3:23).

But people on your team may not climb to the highest heights as you expected them to do. *In fact, they may not have the ability to perform at the level you imagined was possible for them.* So keep in mind that your team members are made of flesh just as you are. They are learning, growing, and pressing forward just as you are. Give them the same room to breathe, to grow, and to be human that you would like for yourself.

Unrealistic expectations — whether placed on leaders by followers or on followers by leaders — always lead to disappointment. It's just better to avoid disappointment by staying realistic in how you view people.

DON'T MOVE TOO FAST

It's beneficial for both the team leader and a prospective team member to establish a testing or discovery time — a probationary period in which both leader and follower can find out about each other and discover the pluses and minuses of the other person. This discovery period is also a time when the leader can determine the extent of the newcomer's capabilities. If the probationary period goes well, the leader can then make the decision to enter into this new working relationship with a much fuller knowledge of the person he has selected.

Instituting a testing time for new leaders is simply an exercise of practical wisdom. In our ministry, we have learned the hard way to move slowly and meticulously when choosing newcomers to our leadership team.

> Instituting a testing time for new leaders is simply an exercise of practical wisdom.

You see, fast decisions are usually wrong decisions. This issue of determining who is supposed to be a part of your team is too serious for you to move quickly. Lives are involved, so take your time and be certain that both you and the newcomer feel compatible with each other.

THE HEART IS THE PRIMARY ISSUE

When choosing people for promotion, it's important to understand that nothing is more important to God in the life of a leader than his *heart*. The heart takes first place over gifts, talents, education, and everything else.

The heart is always the issue with God. That's why He has often chosen people who were less experienced, less educated, and less impressive than others. Although they were less when compared to others, their hearts made them a perfect fit for the purposes of God. The condition of a person's heart always takes first priority above everything else.

(I encourage you to read my book, *If You Were God, Would You Choose You?* This book will encourage you to reach out and take hold of God's call on your life. It clearly establishes that God looks at a person's heart more than anything else when He looks for someone to use.)

CALLED, BUT NOT READY

It's also important to understand that people who are definitely called by God may not yet be prepared or ready to step out and fulfill that divine call. Perhaps the timing isn't right. Perhaps they have problems in their home life that need to be dealt with before they can take the big leap into full-time ministry or leadership. Maybe they are talented and gifted according to the flesh, but they struggle with submitting to authority and shouldn't be used until that battle is conquered. It may be that they are difficult to work with and need to learn how to "give and take" with other people.

Sometimes people are obviously God-called, but their confidence level isn't what it needs to be yet. A leader should be very aware that if he pushes people like that too hard and too fast, he could end up hurting them by giving them levels of responsibility they don't feel confident enough to handle yet.

Unfortunately, I've personally made this mistake of pushing people too hard *and* too fast on several occasions. It was an expensive lesson for me and for the person I was trying to elevate too quickly.

You see, just because someone is "called" doesn't mean he is ready to step into that call. Timing is a very important factor when you are considering whether or not to promote someone to a higher level of authority and responsibility.

> **Just because someone is "called" doesn't mean he is ready to step into that call.**

All these factors are crucial to consider when selecting a person for a responsible position on your leadership team. But above all, to the best of your ability, you should strive to understand a person's heart and attitudes before you bring him or her into your team.

WHAT'S INSIDE A PERSON EVENTUALLY COMES OUT

You and I cannot see a person's heart the way Jesus can, but we *can* see a person's actions and discern his attitudes. Jesus gave us a clue when He said, "...out of the abundance of the heart the mouth speaketh" (Matthew 12:34).

According to Jesus, it isn't difficult to determine what's inside a person's heart. Just listen to him talk. Even if he is eloquent and careful, his mouth will eventually give him away.

Jesus clearly taught that what is inside a person's heart eventually comes to the surface. There is no law of gravity powerful enough to permanently hold down a person's thoughts, feelings, and convictions. Even if that person tries to hide his real feelings and attitudes, sooner or later they will be revealed by his words and actions.

You can count on it: What is inside a man eventually comes out. When it does come out, don't ignore what you're hearing or experiencing because 99% of the time, it will reveal what's really inside that person's heart. Pay attention to what he says, how he responds, and how he acts toward other people. All these are tell-tale signs revealing what you will actually get if you invite that person to become a part of your team.

Many times Denise and I have struggled over the issue of who *is* and who *isn't* ready for a new key position. The issue is *not* whether or not a person is called, but whether or not he is *ready* to step into that calling at that particular time.

> **When you see certain negative attitudes in a prospective leader, those attitudes are like warning signs to slow down, back up, and take a little more time before you lay your hands on that person.**

Even the apostle Paul was called long before God separated him to his position in the Body of Christ. But sometimes Denise and I have deemed a person ready, only to later see attitudes in his or her life that disturbed us deeply.

Everyone needs to constantly work to improve his or her attitudes. But when you see certain negative attitudes in a prospective leader, those attitudes are like warning signs to slow down, back up, and take a little more time before you lay your hands on that person. Attitudes such as the following can lead to behavior that hurts the entire team:

- Rebellion to authority.

- Serving only when it's convenient.

- Constantly inconveniencing other people by being late or tardy for meetings.

- Not being able to get along with other people.

- Sitting and watching while others serve.

- Demonstrating self-centeredness in the way he makes his choices for his division of the ministry.

These are seriously wrong attitudes that almost always indicate you are dealing with a person who has a defective character and who will eventually create some kind of mess or conflict in your ministry.

Too often Denise and I have made the mistake of over-looking glaring defects in a person because we saw his gifts and talents and believed in his potential. Then later we regretted that we talked ourselves into believing such a difficult person could become an asset to our ministry with a little coaching on our part. We should have paid attention to what we were seeing and hearing because it was a clear sign to alert us to the condition of that person's heart.

Over the years we've learned that *most of the time, what you see really is what you get.*

THE TRUTH IS IN THE FRUIT

In Matthew 7:16-20, Jesus taught us that if the tree is *good,* the fruit will be *good.* If the tree is *bad,* the fruit will be *bad.*

A good tree *cannot* produce bad fruit, and a bad tree *cannot* produce good fruit. Good fruit belongs to good trees, and bad fruit belongs to bad trees. It's that simple. The fruit *never* lies.

But how often do we spend time looking at the tree instead of the fruit? The tree may be tall, impressive, stout, and strong. But that impressive-looking tree may produce deadly fruit. Or perhaps the tree will produce good fruit in the future. Regardless, the time for picking its fruit hasn't come yet. In fact, if you pick it before it's ready, it will produce a bitter taste.

Take apples, for example. If you pick good apples too early, their taste is sour, bitter, and sharp. By picking the apple before it's ripe, you ruin what would have been a perfectly good apple. Timing is very important when it comes to harvesting good fruit.

> Don't push a person into a position he isn't ready to handle, or both of you will end up regretting a sour experience.

It's the same way with people. If you pull someone off the pew and plop him into a leadership position before he's ripe, it won't be an enjoyable experience for either you or that person. If he isn't ripe yet, there's nothing *you* can do to make him ripen faster. He just isn't ripe yet. Don't push that person into a position he isn't ready to handle, or both of you will end up regretting a sour experience.

A good example of what I'm talking about is John Mark.

This young man had so much potential that Paul and Barnabas took him with them when they first began their journeys (Acts 13:5). But Acts 13:13 tells us that for some reason, John

Mark abandoned the apostles at an early stage of the trip and returned home to Jerusalem.

The Bible doesn't tell us exactly why John Mark left. Perhaps he was homesick and therefore turned back to Jerusalem. Maybe he was simply immature and unfaithful. Whatever caused John Mark to decide to leave, the experience left such a bitter taste in Paul's mouth that when Barnabas wanted to take this young man on the next trip, Paul *refused.*

Apparently Paul's memories of John Mark were so bitter that he angrily fought with Barnabas about it. Paul even broke up his partnership with Barnabas rather than be subjected to another bad experience with this young man. Whatever John Mark's reason had been for abandoning the apostles, Paul must have considered it a very poor excuse, for at this point he seemed to view the young man with contempt.

But then something truly amazing happened. Years later, Paul wrote in his second epistle to Timothy: "...Take Mark, and bring him with thee: for he is profitable to me for the ministry" (2 Timothy 4:11).

This "Mark" was the same John Mark that Paul earlier refused to take as a part of his team. But by the time Paul wrote those words, he considered this young man not only ready to be used, but "profitable for the ministry"!

It appears that when John Mark went on that first trip with Paul and Barnabas, he was not ready to be used as a part of such a significant leadership team. But later the same man who produced such a bitter taste in Paul's mouth was the person Paul wanted to see.

As is often the case, the problem with John Mark years before wasn't a matter of whether or not he was "called." It was an issue of timing. He wasn't mature enough for heavy-duty ministry at that earlier time. But years had passed, and he had become not only ready, but profitable to the work of God.

LEADERSHIP MUST ACCEPT RESPONSIBILITY FOR THOSE APPOINTED TO KEY POSITIONS

John Mark was like an apple that had been picked too early. His fruit wasn't ready or ripe for picking. That's why it left a bitter taste in Paul's mouth. But the truth is, it wasn't entirely John Mark's fault. Those who chose him to be a part of that first team made a mistake by selecting him too soon. They needed to accept part of the responsibility for putting an immature person in the ministry before he was ready.

I saw another example of "an apple picked too early" several years ago while working with a Christian organization that had serious leadership problems. The man in charge wasn't ready for that kind of assignment. He had personal problems — personal debts that were being ignored and a family life that wasn't in order. Yes, the man was willing to be used and wanted to fulfill his leadership responsibilities. But all the warning signs were flashing, *"Don't put this person in charge! He isn't ready yet!"*

The day came when this individual suddenly and publicly announced his resignation, saying that he refused to work any longer with that organization. The problem was, he hadn't forewarned anyone that he was going to do this! It was a shock to the entire organization.

The staff was in shock, and everyone was scrambling to make sense out of what was happening. Unfortunately, decisions were too quickly made in an attempt to salvage the situation from chaos. As a result of making these decisions too fast, additional critically wrong choices were made that affected the ultimate outreach of the entire organization.

Everyone wanted to blame the man who had abruptly resigned for all the subsequent problems. Certainly, his behavior *was* wrong and horribly immature. But those who had put this man in charge despite all his known problems needed to bear part of the responsibility for what happened. It wasn't just his fault. He should never have been given that position in the first place. His life clearly demonstrated that he wasn't ready for that kind of responsibility in the ministry.

Jesus said that when choosing someone for leadership, we are to consider the *fruit* in his life. It doesn't matter how willing or eager the person is to serve, the fruit that person produces in his personal life and in his attitudes is exactly what you're going to get when you put him in a position of leadership.

So don't ignore what you see! Don't overlook the warning signs that are flashing all around you! If you send this person out too quickly or accept him as a member of your team before he is ready, you *must* bear the responsibility for what happens if a storm develops all around him.

Jesus said, "Wherefore by their fruits ye shall know them" (Matthew 7:20). We must be very careful to look at the fruit of people's lives when we consider them for key positions in our churches or ministries. The outward fruit is the byproduct of the tree's inner sap. That sap produces the tree's foliage and fruit.

In the same way, a person's attitude is like the sap of a tree. It comes *directly* from inside him. And just as the sap of a tree produces good or bad fruit, a person's inner thoughts and attitudes will be manifested in his outward attitudes and actions. So if you want to know what's inside a person, just observe his attitudes and watch how he relates to other people. His *fruit* will tell you the truth about who he really is.

THE REASON I'VE WRITTEN THIS BOOK

As the leader of our ministry, I am confronted with a challenge — *the same challenge every pastor or leader of a ministry or organization is confronted with.* Because I can't see what's inside a person's heart, I find it necessary to pay careful attention to what comes out of that person when he's placed in different situations. His reactions help me determine the condition of his heart, and that helps me know if I want him to be a team player in our ministry.

Many people find themselves in the same position I'm in. They are the ones who must decide who is chosen for a leadership position and who is not. I've written this book to help leaders faced with this dilemma form an opinion about who *should* and who *shouldn't* be selected for those positions of responsibility. This book will also help the reader who is asking himself if *he* is ready for a spiritual promotion.

So let's move on to look at my ten practical guidelines for determining if a person is ready to be a part of your team. You may find them to be somewhat confrontational and aggressive. But I present them to you as guidelines I have personally used in the development of my own ministry in the former Soviet Union. I've found that following these ten points helps me make wise choices. God may give you other ways to determine if a person is ready for leadership, but these guidelines have been helpful in our particular ministry.

As you consider these suggestions in regard to potential leaders, remember that *people are people.* You will never find a perfect person. In fact, if those same people you're testing turned the test around and applied it to *you,* you might discover your scores aren't all that perfect either! So don't forget to let mercy play a role in your selection process!

These suggested tests are not intended to turn you into a "Pharisee" who suddenly starts digging for dirt in other people's lives. Rather, they are simply meant to serve as a guide to help you take a more serious look at people before you lay your hands on them and give them public approval.

As you examine prospective leaders, remember to look for their strengths as well as their weaknesses; then be sure to *magnify* their strengths. You may find a person who has proven character but perhaps one or two defects here and there as well. In that case, learn to balance the defects with the character you've seen in other areas of his or her life.

In most cases, you'll find people have more strengths than they do weaknesses. Most often their weaknesses are small inconsistencies based on fears they have about stepping out in faith to assume greater roles of responsibility. These areas are correctable as long as they have an open, teachable heart and are submitted to your authority.

In the final analysis, you must learn to develop discernment from the Spirit of God about whom you should and should not use in your team of leaders. If you will carefully listen to the voice of the Holy Spirit and use the type of character tests I suggest in the following chapters, you will make very few mistakes in selecting leadership.

Go slowly. Move deliberately. Look carefully. Then act with confidence when you are finally ready to select a leader. If you act fast, you'll be sorry later. Take your time so you can feel good about your choices.

QUESTIONS FOR PERSONAL GROWTH OR GROUP DISCUSSION

1. What should your response be when you discover certain flaws or imperfections in the life of a person whom God has placed over you?

2. What kind of instructions should you give your own prospective leaders in order to prepare them to work with you with the proper attitude when they see *your* imperfections?

3. What would be a wise course of action to take when someone in authority places unrealistic expectations on you?

4. As a leader, how should you respond when someone under you claims that you are placing unrealistic expectations on him or her?

5. What is one primary test in determining whether someone with a strong call to leadership on his or her life is ready to step into that position of leadership?

NOTES:

_____

_____

_____

_____

_____

_____

_____

_____

_____

_____

_____

_____

_____

_____

_____

_____

_____

_____

_____

_____

WATCH TO SEE IF
THE POTENTIAL LEADER
HAS DESIRE

*E*very person dreams to succeed. Every church prays to grow. Every business and organization wants to realize its business or social goals. *God puts it in the heart of man to do something great!*

It's a thrilling experience to take your church higher or to lead your business or organization to the pinnacle of success. But to attain that measure of success, you will probably have to climb a few mountains. And making it to the top of those mountains will require an incredible amount of *desire.*

Even though every person has a dream for success, that doesn't mean every person will attain it. It takes great effort and hard work to achieve success in any realm of life. Many people who dream of success will never experience it because they don't desire it enough; therefore, they aren't willing to put forth the effort to make it happen.

Proverbs 28:19 *(NIV)* presents a principle along this line that's so basic, many people overlook it. It says, "He who works his land will have abundant food, but the one who chases fantasies will have his fill of poverty." This very simple principle promises that those who work hard and put their full energies into their assignment will be abundantly and richly blessed.

> Those who work hard and put their full energies into their assignment will be abundantly and richly blessed.

I have held on to this Bible verse all my life. You see, I was born into a German heritage. My family members always believed in hard work. When they committed themselves to do a project, they were committed to the end — and they believed that whatever they set out to do had to be done with excellence.

One look at my parents' house told the whole story about our family. The yard was always mowed, the sidewalks perfectly edged, and the trees and bushes nicely trimmed. The flowerbed was also full of beautiful, blossoming flowers. My grandfather Renner's house looked the same — always immaculate in appearance. In fact, it was so clean inside his house, you could have eaten off the floor!

I thank God that I was reared in a home where this kind of excellence was expected. My parents loved me and my sisters enough to give us this example, and they disciplined us to know that this was the standard expected of us in life. However, as a human being dressed in flesh, I've still had those moments when my flesh wanted to vegetate — to do nothing but sit around and waste precious time.

But doing nothing results in nothing. If I want to reap glorious results and achieve grandiose victories in my life, I'll have to put in the effort to make it happen. Knowing this is the case, I've built my work ethic on the principle and promise of Proverbs 28:19. *God promises that if I work, I'll be blessed.* It's just that simple.

WATCH OUT FOR 'FANTASY-CHASERS'

But Proverbs 28:19 *(NIV)* also says that "...the one who chases fantasies will have his fill of poverty." Who are these *fantasy-chasers* this verse is speaking about?

Fantasy-chasers are those who dream of success but never do a thing to achieve it. They sit at home doing nothing significant with their lives. Yet all the while they fantasize about how someday they'll get a big break and success will arrive at their doorstep.

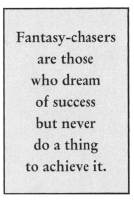

Fantasy-chasers are those who dream of success but never do a thing to achieve it.

This isn't just a harmless fantasy; it's as unreal as the hallucinations of someone on drugs! These people talk of success, dream of success, and wait for success. But they can kiss this mirage good-bye, because if they're not willing to get up, get to work, and put out the effort to attain their goals, their dream of success will never come to pass. It is reduced to nothing more than a *fantasy*.

There's a major difference between the two basic types of dreamers. One person dreams, and he works very hard to achieve his dream. The other person also dreams, but he does nothing to fulfill his dreams except fantasize and indulge in wishful thinking about the future. Although these two types of dreamers are different in many ways, one big inward difference between them is their level of *desire*. Desire is an intense, inward appetite for something — a hunger, craving, longing, or thirst that causes a person to yearn and lust for a certain goal or object. This inward desire is so strong that it becomes a driving aspiration, an all-consuming ambition that doesn't know how to stop until it obtains the coveted prize. Desire can become so powerful that it literally compels the person to get up and take the necessary action to make his dream come to pass.

I often hear Christians say that people who are "ambitious" are carnal and unspiritual. I have especially heard this over the years in the territory of the former Soviet Union. I'd like to correct this thinking right now.

It's true that carnal ambition should have no place in the Church. I'm talking about *the kind of ambition that creates a spirit of competition between members of the Body of Christ. But there is also a godly ambition — an ambition to be the best, highest, finest, and most superb example of whatever one is called to do.* This ambition for excellence is the right kind of ambition — but regrettably, it is also the kind that is greatly lacking in the Body of Christ.

It's a sad fact that much of what is done in Jesus' Name is average, mundane, unimpressive, ordinary, and even banal. It ought to be just the opposite! As Christians who are indwelt by the Spirit of God, we should produce the most impressive, stimulating, exhilarating, inspiring, and rousing work on planet earth! *Nothing should be done better than the way a Christian does it.*

However, Christians are sinners saved by grace, and too often they carry the residual of carnal thinking and wrong behavior into their new Christian life, even though they are now blood-washed and indwelt by the Holy Spirit. Their inner man is alive to God, but their mind is still unrenewed. As part of the renewal process, they must develop a new work ethic and higher level of expectation for themselves. They have to get rid of the laziness that has strapped them to defeat, mediocrity, and a poverty mentality.

I am confronted by this mediocre way of thinking all the time as I work in the former Soviet Union. I am amazed at the low standards that people accept and even perceive to be normal.

For example, why should any believer live in an apartment that has wallpaper falling off the walls? I understand that people may have a money problem that keeps them from buying new wallpaper. But nothing is stopping them from gluing that old wallpaper back on the wall again! Why should they be satisfied to live in such low-standard conditions?

And this isn't just true of people in the former Soviet Union. As I travel and preach all over the world, I am often astonished at the low standards accepted as "normal." Even in the United States, I frequently minister in churches where it looks like nothing has been organized since the day those churches opened!

Brochures and leaflets are scattered all over tables as if someone deliberately messed them up. The bathrooms are dirty and lack toilet paper, soap, and paper towels so people can dry their hands. Trash cans are so full, they look like they haven't been emptied in weeks. The song lyrics written on overhead projector sheets for worship are misspelled, crossed out, or written so sloppily that it should be an embarrassment to the whole church. Yet all these things are overlooked as if disorder and sloppiness were normal qualities to be found in the local church.

> **One thing is absolutely sure: What you have inside of you is exactly what you will impart to others.**

But mediocre standards are *not* normal. It's all an issue of desire. Some have a great desire for excellence in life, and others do not.

One thing is absolutely sure: *What you have inside of you is exactly what you will impart to others.*

So don't put a person in charge of a department in your church, ministry, or organization who is content to live a low-level existence at home. Why? Because that's exactly what you can expect him to give to that department over which you've made him a leader. *A person can give only what he has inside of himself.*

If a person's standards are low in his personal life, he will replicate those same low standards in the part of the ministry or organization that has been placed under his authority. You *can't* expect anything more because *he just can't give what he doesn't have.* If he's content with a mediocre level of desire or a mediocre way of thinking, that is exactly what he will be able to impart to others.

This lack of desire is the reason why so much of what is done in the Christian world is of such inferior quality. A person

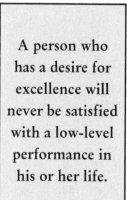

> **A person who has a desire for excellence will never be satisfied with a low-level performance in his or her life.**

who is satisfied with little will never achieve much. On the other hand, *a person who has a desire for excellence will never be satisfied with a low-level performance in his or her life.*

THE MOST IMPORTANT QUALIFICATION
FOR LEADERSHIP

In First Timothy 3, the apostle Paul instructed Timothy on how to choose leaders for his church in Ephesus. As Paul began listing character qualifications that every leader must have, the first quality he listed as supremely important for leadership was "desire" (1 Timothy 3:1).

The word "desire" is the Greek word *orgidzo.* It describes *a longing, craving, urge, burning desire, or yearning ambition to achieve something or to become something.* It portrays *a person so fixed on the object of his desire that his whole being is stretched forward to take hold of that goal or object.*

Paul put the qualification of desire as foremost above anything else on his list of requirements for leaders. It takes only a few personal experiences with desireless people to make it perfectly clear why Paul did this!

Through the years, I've learned the wisdom of looking for people who have desire. There is nothing more dreadful or irritating than to have a supposed leader on the team who doesn't even possess enough initiative to get up and do his job.

One of the greatest frustrations I've experienced through the years is working with people who have great potential but are apathetic about life. It's even more frustrating when these people grew up in Christian homes and should therefore have been taught to pursue a higher standard for life.

However, many people weren't raised according to a high standard of excellence as my parents raised me. Therefore, these people don't possess a deep desire to be excellent in everything they do. They grew up in an environment where low-level thinking was viewed as normal, so that's the standard they've accepted for their own lives. However, a person who comes from a low-level background hurts only himself when he uses that as an excuse for staying mediocre.

It's so frustrating when people have the opportunity to learn, to adapt, and to better themselves, but they don't take advantage of these opportunities and therefore never experience needed change. You can send them to school, educate them, and even pay for them to fly halfway around the world in order to learn new and better techniques. But if they don't possess the inner drive to become better and more professional, it doesn't matter how much time or money you throw at them. It's all a waste unless they have *desire*.

Desireless people just don't seem to care. They often appear:

- UNCONCERNED — They have no driving motivation to be concerned about anything.

- UNEMOTIONAL — They don't have enough passion to feel emotion about what they're doing.

- INDIFFERENT — They often have a "take it or leave it" mentality.

- NONCHALANT — They are of the opinion, "What will be will be, so why try to do anything about it?"

- UNRESPONSIVE — They often sit and look at you when you're talking to them as if you haven't said a word.

- DETACHED — They are not genuinely connected to any kind of commitment.

- LETHARGIC — They're so lazy, they look like they don't have enough energy to get off the pew!

- INACTIVE — They come to church, but don't ask them to do anything because they don't have a heart to serve or to be regularly active in anything that requires effort.

Desireless people stroll through life at their own pace, accepting standards and practices that would *never* be accepted in the business or secular world. As a result, a large portion of the lost world looks at the Church as a pathetic entity made up of a bunch of nincompoops who aren't serious about what they do or say.

Not too long ago, I met with a head of government. This man told me, "I just don't understand these Christians. They say they love the Lord so much, but they are the laziest people I've ever met in my life. I'm amazed that anyone would be satisfied to live with such low standards."

I found myself wanting to apologize for the Body of Christ. The truth is, I've held the same opinion on many occasions when I've confronted talented, gifted, knowledgeable believers who didn't have even enough gumption to get up and do something valuable with their lives. It's a mystery to me how someone can claim to be indwelt by the Spirit of God, yet be satisfied with a low-level existence.

Desireless people are like *dead people!* You push, shove, beg, plead, and pray for them to get involved in Kingdom work. Finally, they respond to your constant requests and volunteer to do something in the church. They even do it for a while — at least until they feel a little opposition or are just too tired to come to church. At that point, they give up.

> It's a mystery to me how someone can claim to be indwelt by the Spirit of God, yet be satisfied with a low-level existence.

These people don't have enough *desire* to make it through the obstacles they face along the way. This is another reason a potential leader must demonstrate this quality of strong inward desire.

Obstacles will come as you grow in the Lord. From time to time, hindrances will try to knock you out of your spiritual race. If you don't have a strong desire to be used by God, it won't take too many of these obstacles and hindrances to make you give up and back out of your commitments. That's why it's essential to develop an inner desire strong enough to overcome the forces that come against you along the way.

> It's essential to develop an inner desire strong enough to overcome the forces that come against you along the way.

We have a young man in our church who is so full of desire that he finds himself right in the middle of everything — *even in the middle of things he shouldn't be involved in.* He's so aggressive in his efforts to be involved that he even upsets some of our top team members. I've heard them complain, "Why is he in the middle of everything all the time?"

But I have mercy on this young man because he reminds me of myself when I was his age. I wanted to be used by God so much that it consumed me. I didn't care what I was asked to do, where I was asked to sit or stand, or how low or menial the task was that was given me — I just wanted to be *used*.

I wanted to prophesy, preach, testify, or do anything else that could be done for the Lord. I was like a walking bomb of desire — just waiting to explode for God at any moment.

As I watch this young man today, I see myself two decades ago. His intense desire tells me that he will eventually become a mighty instrument in the hands of God. He may do immature things now and then, but it's easier to correct some-

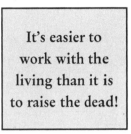

It's easier to work with the living than it is to raise the dead!

one like him than it is to try to use someone who has no desire at all. *Believe me, it's easier to work with the living than it is to raise the dead!*

PEOPLE WHO DO JUST THE MINIMUM

> **Any person who does just the required minimum should *never* be considered for leadership.**

Any person who does just the required minimum should *never* be considered for leadership. Therefore, ask a potential leader to get very involved in the work that needs to be done.

If there's a need and no one else is meeting it, you should expect that person to step forward to fill that position. Watch to see if he jumps in without being asked. You shouldn't have to beg and plead with anyone. This is part of the responsibility of leadership.

If that person just sits and watches as a need goes unmet, you either need to correct him or stop praying about whether or not he should be used as a leader. If he wants to lead, *then let him lead.* He should be on his feet and ready at any moment to do whatever is needed.

One Sunday morning a lady had a heart problem in one of our church services. Someone in the congregation called out and asked for help. I watched as supposed leaders looked around to see who would step forward to help. No one responded. Finally, I said to them, *"If you're going to lead, then get up on your feet and do your job! Why is everyone just sitting and looking at everyone else?"*

Leaders should be on their feet the instant a need arises. That kind of immediate response reveals that they are *serious* and *professional* in their responsibilities. And if no one else is available to do the job, the person who is aspiring to be a leader should volunteer to do it!

> How a person responds when unexpected needs arise often reveals the intensity of his ambition or desire to be in the inner ring of leadership.

How a person responds when unexpected needs arise often reveals the intensity of his ambition or desire to be in the inner ring of leadership. If he's happy to sit on the sidelines and watch everyone else play the game, don't invite him to be on your team. He isn't ready to be a team player yet.

YOUR LEADERS WILL REPRODUCE
WHAT THEY ARE THEMSELVES

Because of my own personal encounters with desireless people, I understand why Paul put *desire* at the top of his list of leadership qualifications. Timothy was in the midst of a leadership selection process in his church, and Paul wrote him a letter to help him make right choices. I'm sure Paul had experienced low-level believers in the course of his own ministry. Therefore, he didn't want Timothy (or you and me!) to make the mistake of putting desireless people into powerful positions of leadership.

Psalm 133:1,2 teaches us the principle I mentioned earlier — that whatever is on the head is *exactly* what will flow down to affect the rest of the body. This means if you put a desireless person in charge of a division of your ministry, his low-level desire is exactly what will be replicated in that entire division. Therefore, you better choose your leaders wisely because whatever is inside them is *precisely* what they are going to reproduce.

As the head of our organization, I look very carefully at a person before I give him great responsibility or invite him to be a part of our team. I want to know the standards he maintains in his own personal life. Yes, I look at spiritual issues too. But many times it's the practical areas of life that tell the real story about what kind of person a potential candidate is.

So be very careful not to overspiritualize the selection process when choosing leaders. Don't ignore telltale signs in a candidate's natural life that alert you to a lack of desire.

If I'm going to invite a person into my leadership team, I want to really know exactly whom I am getting. So in addition to observing how well the person prays, prophesies, or preaches, I also ask:

- Is his home or apartment clean?

- Does he drive an automobile that's littered with dirt and debris? Would I be comfortable riding across town in his car without worrying about getting covered with cat or dog hair?

- Does he pay his bills on time?

- Does he iron his clothes, or is he content to walk around in wrinkled clothing?

- How clean are this person's fingernails? Do they always look like he just crawled out from under his car?

- Are his shoes polished, or are they scraped and scuffed beyond salvaging?

- Does he show up to appointments and meetings on time, or is he regularly late, always giving some excuse for why he couldn't get there on time?

- If the candidate is a man, does he shave before he shows up at meetings, or does he look shabby and unkempt?

- If the candidate is a woman, does she give attention to her hair and maintain a well-groomed appearance?

I want to repeat: Whatever a person has inside him is exactly what he will replicate in his or her division of the ministry. You may not believe me now, but just give yourself a little time and experience in the ministry, and you'll find out the truth of this principle.

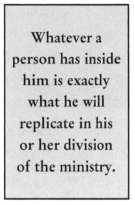

Whatever a person has inside him is exactly what he will replicate in his or her division of the ministry.

Let me give you an example from my own ministry. We once had a youth pastor who was excellent in everything he did. It didn't matter what task he set out to accomplish, I always knew it would be done with excellence: He demonstrated time and again the high level of expectation he maintained for himself and others. His office was neat, his youth group was orderly, and his entire division of the ministry reflected genuine care and concern.

Once when my family was visiting in the United States and I was by myself on the other side of the ocean, this youth minister invited me to come stay with him a few days so we could enjoy some good fellowship. I had wanted to spend some quality time with the young man, so I agreed.

When I entered this youth minister's home, I was amazed. It was so clean. Towels were nicely hung in the kitchen. The items in the refrigerator looked like they were perfectly arranged in a special kind of order. Shoes were neatly ordered in the entry foyer.

One morning I asked for a towel before I went into the bathroom to take a shower. He told me the towels were in a certain drawer in the living room, so I went to get one. But instead of opening the towel drawer, I mistakenly opened the drawer where he kept his underwear. I started laughing. Even his items of underwear were perfectly folded and arranged in the drawer!

After two days of staying in this man's home, I understood why his ministry was so well organized. It was just an extension of his private life. How he conducted himself in his personal life was *exactly* what he replicated in his ministry.

Before I went to my youth minister's home for those two days, I could have predicted what I would find there. I knew his private life was ordered and organized because that's what he was producing in his public ministry. I would have been completely shocked if he'd been organized at work and disorganized at home, because what happens at home is *usually* what happens at work.

- If you invite a disorganized person to join your team, he will produce disorganization.

- If a sloppy person joins your team, he will produce a sloppy ministry.

- If you hire a person for a position on your team who doesn't take anything seriously, he will reproduce a frivolous attitude toward ministry.

- If you have a person with low standards on your team, he will produce low standards in his ministry.

- If you invite a desireless person to your team, he will be lazy, sluggish, and unprogressive in carrying out his ministerial responsibilities.

- But if you invite *a person with desire* to your team, he will produce a department full of energy and vitality, and the people under his authority will develop a ferocious appetite to achieve the highest, finest, and best in everything that they do.

I would rather work with a less talented person who has desire than with a talented person who has no desire. What good are a person's gifts and talents if he doesn't have the inward drive to get up and use those gifts for God's glory? It's better to train a young man or woman who doesn't have a lot of experience and is less qualified than others, but who is willing to pay the price, put in the time and effort, and make personal sacrifices to become all that he or she can be.

MY TEAM IN THE FORMER SOVIET UNION

The leadership of my staff in the former USSR may lack the education that is afforded to people in Western nations, but their *desire* to learn and develop their skills makes up for any lack. This trait is what makes me most proud of them.

Regardless of the obstacles my staff members face or the challenges they run up against, they are determined to push through and do what God has called them to do. Their *inward longing, craving, hunger, burning desire, and yearning ambition* is to accomplish something significant for God. That drive — that inward motivation — keeps them going even when things get tough.

Leaders need this ferocious desire because they *will* run into obstacles and challenges along the way. If their desire is small or weak, it won't take a very strong attack from the devil to knock them out of the race.

But when a person is so desirous to become all God wants him to be that he refuses to quit, that person is going to become someone in the Kingdom of God! Desire propels people like that forward to become more than they are right now. This desire may even manifest as *dissatisfaction* because they aren't willing to remain stuck at their current level of living, never moving beyond the status quo.

My associate is one of those people who desires to be the best. He strives for excellence both in his personal appearance and in the way his home is kept and managed. His standard of excellence is also manifested in the way he fulfills his job responsibilities and in his high expectations for the people who serve in our ministry.

Years ago when my associate and I first started working together, I became frustrated with him because nothing ever seemed to please him. Whether the subject under discussion was the choir, the ushers, the Sunday school teachers, the youth ministry, or special church programs and presentations, nothing ever seemed to attain his level of expectation.

Even when I was thrilled with a special performance in the church or with a certain church department, my associate always seemed displeased, discontented, and disappointed. At times he even seemed exasperated, bothered, aggravated, and annoyed that things were not done on a higher level. He never verbalized his disappointments to the people, but he privately confided to me how he wanted so much more for our church than what he was seeing. To the people, he seemed satisfied. But privately, I heard about his inner struggles because things were not being done on a higher level.

It took some time, but finally I came to understand my associate's reactions and emotions. His desire for excellence was so great that he couldn't bear the thought of God's people performing at less than the highest level possible. This inward desire to be the best wouldn't allow him to be satisfied with anything less than the highest standard of service and performance.

My associate's feelings weren't negative or nit-picky. They were a manifestation of his deep, inner *desire* for excellence — a desire that caused him to refuse to accept anything less than *the best* for God's Kingdom.

Working with strong team leaders such as my associate has taught me that desire is often reflected in the way a person takes responsibility for the task assigned to him. If he embraces his work as if it belongs to him — putting his whole heart into the task of making it even better — this is a powerful sign that he could become a responsible, committed leader.

Today when I work in our Moscow office, I'm thrilled to see the way that entire staff has embraced the call of God and how they feel a sense of "ownership" with what they do. It isn't just *my* ministry they're managing; they look at it as *their* ministry too. Every staff member is filled with an intense *desire* to do his or her best, to reach the most people, and to operate in the most effective manner for the Kingdom of God.

Pay attention when you find people who demonstrate this kind of loyalty and fierce determination to be used in your ministry; who refuse to be easily moved; and who will not give up. The fact that they are so determined probably means they have the kind of desire you're looking for in your potential leaders.

MANY OBSTACLES TO OVERCOME

When a person begins the process of becoming a leader, he will inevitably face many obstacles along the way. There will also be multitudes of mountains a new leader has to scale in order to make it to the top and back down the other side.

One mountain every potential leader has to climb is learning how to submit to authority and receive correction. This is a difficult challenge for anyone.

I remember when I was younger and just getting started in the ministry, my pastor would occasionally call me in for a "visit." I knew that always meant I was in trouble for something.

My flesh wanted to defend itself, fight for its rights, and put up a fight. But the Lord began to teach me that I was to submit to that pastor's authority and receive his correction, even if I didn't like or agree with what he said. That was a huge mountain for me to scale.

Another mountain every leader faces is learning to deal with people. People can be difficult sometimes. After a leader serves them to the best of his ability and gives them all he has to give of himself, they can "stab him in the back" and act ungrateful. That can be very hard to handle emotionally. If a leader doesn't quickly take control of his soul, the devil will try to sow seeds of resentment and offense into his heart. So learning to serve people with a joyful heart — regardless of how they do or do not respond — is another mountain every leader must learn to scale.

Another big mountain a new leader may face along the way is finding the needed finances to do what God has told him to do. Personally, I've never had the money to do anything God has called me to do at the onset of the task or project. But who needs money? All I need is a word from God.

If you'll obey what God has told you to do, your obedience will work like a magnet. It will bring you all the cash needed to accomplish that job all the way to its conclusion. But when you first start your life of faith and obedience, a lack of cash may seem insurmountable to you. You can do it. You can overcome it. But you'll have to learn how to deal with this type of mountain by actually scaling each one that looms in your path. With a little experience and success, you'll soon learn that money is not a problem for God.

You and your team members will face all kinds of mountains during the course of your ministry. To make it up and over each of these challenges (which are too many to list here!), you will all need *desire.* If you have desire that is stronger than any obstacle, tenacious in its will to achieve, unwavering in its commitment to keep going until the job is complete, resolute and stalwart in its stand — then you'll always overcome the problems you face and you'll always end up the winner.

> Without an inward desire that is stronger than the opposing forces that are certain to come against you, you are in for a heap of trouble.

But if you lack this unwavering, tenacious, resolute, and stalwart desire, it won't take too much to knock you down, knock you out, or even throw you clear out of the ring. One little push from the enemy, and you'll give up. The first time you encounter a little opposition and resistance, you'll go scrambling back to your comfort zone where you feel safe and secure. Without an inward desire that is stronger than the opposing forces that are certain to come against you, you are in for a heap of trouble.

Since it's inevitable that your potential leaders will face many challenges and mountains along the way, you may as well urge them to mentally put on their climbing gear. They'll have to get ready to scale those mountains if they plan on getting to the other side! And they better have sufficient desire to make it all the way to the top, or they'll never get there. *It takes strong desire to be the best!*

It Takes Desire To Get to the Top

Years ago I found out through hard experience the important role that desire plays in making it to the top of a mountain — only in this case, the mountain was a real one!

One day I saw a photograph taken from the summit of one of Canada's tallest mountains. It was the most beautiful photograph I had ever seen. In fact, it was such an amazing sight that I determined I would personally take a trip to Canada and climb to the top of that summit to see the view in real life!

Seeing that photograph stirred me to action. The more I thought about it, the more I *desired* to make it to the top of that mountain myself. A mental vision of me reaching the summit of that mountain filled my thoughts. I had watched television programs about mountain climbers and had always been interested in that type of daring activity. Now I was no longer content just to think about it — I wanted to do it *myself.*

To get ready for the climb, I went on a diet and lost a lot of weight. I read books about mountain climbing and about the Canadian Rockies mountain range. Finally, I traveled to Canada, where I met with a group of men from a Canadian church who would accompany me to the top of the mountain.

All the other men were climbers. *I was not.* They were in superb physical condition. *I was not.* I had no idea how difficult the journey was going to be. But I had enough *desire* to keep me going and get me to the top!

A week before the climb, a brother in the Lord came to me after a church service I was conducting in the state of Kansas. He gave me a giant hug and said, "Brother Rick, thank you for your ministry. God used you to change my life!" I was thrilled with his testimony, but he hugged me so tightly that he broke a rib in my left side!

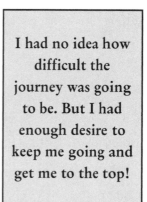

I had no idea how difficult the journey was going to be. But I had enough desire to keep me going and get me to the top!

The pain was excruciating. At night as I slept, I cringed every time I tried to roll from one side to the other. When I tried to lift a sack of groceries from the car to carry them into the house, the pain was horrific!

As Denise and I drove across the states of Colorado, Wyoming, and Montana on our way to Canada, she kept pleading, *"Rick, you shouldn't try to make that climb with a broken rib!"*

But no broken rib was going to stop me! I was so full of desire that I was determined to make it to the top of that mountain peak. With a broken rib, an unfit physique, and a backpack loaded with seventy-five pounds of supplies, I looked to the top of that mountain and said, *"Here I come!"*

So we began the difficult ascent. It wasn't the most dangerous climb, but it *could* be dangerous to a person unfamiliar with mountains. It could be *very dangerous* to a person as "unfit" as I was! It was treacherous enough to have claimed the lives of several people through the years.

In fact, just days before our own climb, two professional climbers tried to cross a patch of black ice at the same spot where we were headed. Suddenly they disappeared out of sight as they hurtled several thousand feet down to their deaths on the glacier below!

Sharp ridges and steep cliffs were just a few risks connected with the climb. Altitude sickness was another risk. *Unfortunately for me, it was a risk I knew nothing about!*

I huffed, puffed, and pushed my way to the top of that mountain. With each step, the weight of my backpack got heavier. I scrambled up ninety-degree inclines that led to even sharper inclines. Rocks tumbled under my feet. I fell. I rolled. I promised God that I would never attempt to do such a stupid thing again if I could just get to the top and back down alive!

As I held on to a ragged rock to keep from falling, I noticed a mountain goat watching me! It looked at me as if to say, *"What in the world are you doing up here?"*

I wondered, *Do I look as stupid to that goat as I look to myself?*

What in the world was I doing on top of this mountain? It was a world-class climb — and it was my *first* climb! I wished I had known what I was getting into before I started!

A View From the Top
Made It Worth All the Trouble

Finally, I stood on the top of that mountain and looked out over the peaks of the Canadian Rockies.

Spread out before me was a panoramic view of hundreds of incredibly beautiful mountain peaks. The sky was so clear, I could see for a hundred miles. I could see peak after peak after peak. As the sun went down, I watched as orange, blue, and purple tones filled the sky. I'd seen sunsets in California and Hawaii, but this was gorgeous beyond words! The photograph I had seen paled in comparison to the real thing!

My exhaustion disappeared, and for a few minutes, I forgot about the hardships I had encountered to get to the top of the mountain. I had conquered that mountain! I'd really done it! My heart was shouting!

But my great victory was about to be interrupted in a big way by *altitude sickness.* A few hours later, my victorious celebration ended as I began to feel nausea and dizziness come over me. It came fast and hard, wave after wave of nausea pounding against me until I was unable to stand. My eyes began to see black spots. My head seemed to spin round and round, and I started violently vomiting. I vomited and vomited until I had nothing left in my stomach to throw up. Even then, my body still convulsed with dry heaves.

Dehydrated and weak, I didn't know how I could physically make it through the night. All night long my body wrenched with dry heaves, even though my stomach was empty. I cried. I pleaded for help. I prayed. It was a sickness like nothing I had ever experienced in my life.

The next morning I was still sick and so physically weak that I had to work hard to muster up the energy to take a few steps. The problem was that we had to start the trip back down the slopes to where we had begun the climb the day before. The other men didn't know how I was going to make it. But I was determined that the mountain wasn't going to conquer me! I was going to make it up and down that mountain successfully. My desire was stronger than my physical weakness.

I took one small step down the mountain.

Then another small step.

Then another and another.

Each step was such an effort that I had to work up the nerve to take the next small step. A climber from another group who passed me on my way down saw how sick I was and contacted the Canadian Mounties to notify them about my condition. Unknown to me, mountain police began searching the mountain for the dehydrated climber — *me!*

When I reached the bottom, I was met by a host of Canadian Mounties who had been searching the mountain for me. One took me by the arm, led me to a vehicle, and drove me straight to a hostel. On the way, the man made sure I was drinking plenty of fluid. Meanwhile, he lectured me on the dangers of mountain climbing. He let me know how stupid it was for me to attempt that climb without first preparing myself.

The other men in our group already knew the risks. They *assumed* that I knew them too. But I was *uninformed* and *unprepared.* If I had possessed that information, it wouldn't have made the climb easier, but at least I would have understood what I was going to face. Lack of information meant I had to figure it all out on my own. *That is always the hardest way to learn!*

Why am I telling you this story? Because you, too, will run into many obstacles along the way that no one has prepared you to face. It isn't that anyone deliberately denied you the information. People may have assumed that you already understood. They may have wrongly believed that you were more prepared than you were. This is true not only for yourself, but for those you choose to be a part of your team.

But when you or your team members do face unexpected problems that seem impossible to solve, remember what we've been talking about in this chapter.

- *Any obstacle can be overcome.*
- *Any challenge can be conquered.*
- *Any mountain can be successfully climbed — IF you have the inward desire and motivation to achieve your goal.*

This is why desire is such a vital issue when choosing your top leadership team.

WHY PEOPLE FAIL IS USUALLY NOT A MYSTERY

There are concrete reasons why some people succeed and others fail. It isn't always an unexplained mystery. Churches, ministries, organizations, and individuals frequently fail because no one properly informed them about the risks on the journey to spiritual growth. This lack of preparation makes them ill-equipped for the obstacles they inevitably face along the way.

If your level of desire is strong, it doesn't matter if you're ill-equipped in some ways for your assigned task because your inward determination will make up for any lack. Of course, when you make it to the top of your mountain as I did that day in the Canadian Rockies, you may find yourself saying, *"Gee, I'm glad I made it, but it would have been nice if someone had prepared me for what I'd have to deal with on the way up here!"*

This is why I'm emphasizing the fact that when you choose people for your leadership team, you are doing both them and yourself a favor when you make *desire* one of the determining factors for who is and who isn't ready for a spiritual promotion. It wasn't an accident that Paul put desire at the top of the list in First Timothy 3:1. Desire is the chief characteristic *required* for anyone who is going to survive the challenges of ministry and keep serving God and others with a pure heart.

> Desire is the chief characteristic *required* for anyone who is going to survive the challenges of ministry and keep serving God and others with a pure heart.

It's good to have gifted and talented people on the team, but sometimes the most gifted are also lazy and uncommitted. It's far better to have a less talented person who is so loaded with *desire* for excellence that nothing can get in his way to stop him from achieving his goal.

This is the most basic and elementary point for determining who is and who isn't qualified for the next big job assignment. If a person's spiritual desire is only strong enough to carry him through convenient or enjoyable times, his fire won't last long. To be a successful leader, he must demonstrate the kind of desire and commitment that keeps pushing forward until his task is accomplished with the highest level of professionalism he is able to give to it.

QUESTIONS FOR PERSONAL GROWTH OR GROUP DISCUSSION

1. What are the two basic types of dreamers? In the past, which category of dreamer would have best described you? Which describes you today?

2. What is the primary factor that determines whether a person lives by standards of mediocrity or excellence?

3. What steps can you take to develop a strong inner desire to fulfill your God-given assignment?

4. What can you do to help determine whether or not a potential leader is driven by desire in his or her life?

5. What quality is more imperative for overcoming challenges in life and ministry — talent or desire?

NOTES:

_____

_____

_____

_____

_____

_____

_____

_____

_____

_____

_____

_____

_____

_____

_____

_____

_____

_____

_____

_____

DOES THIS PERSON UNDERSTAND THE IMPORTANCE OF COMMUNICATION?

*L*eadership is *communication*. That may sound too simple to be true, but it's a fact that good leaders and bad leaders are distinguished by how they communicate. When it comes to good leadership, *communication is the name of the game.*

Just take a little time to analyze the type of problems that commonly arise within churches, ministries, businesses, and organizations. You'll discover that most of those problems find their roots in *poor communication.*

- Plans are not followed as expected.

- Instructions are not carried out.

- Details get lost along the way.

- Dates for completing projects are not taken seriously.

The pastor or leader becomes frustrated with his staff and workers — and the staff and workers become frustrated that their leader never seems to be satisfied with their performance.

Tensions increase.

Emotions rise.

Tempers flare.

Conflict erupts.

Ill feelings grow between leader and followers.

These are all signs of bad communication. Something is wrong either with how the leader is communicating or with how his staff is listening. Either way, *it's a communication problem.*

My own years of experience have taught me that most people want to please their pastor or director. They want to do a good job. They usually *think* they are doing exactly what they've been asked to do. However, if people think they understand when in reality they don't, it's usually a sign that the leader needs to reassess his methods of communication.

It's normal for people to occasionally misunderstand. But when staff members misunderstand their leader's instructions 99% of the time, something is wrong with the way that leader is communicating with those under his authority. His followers *cannot* be wrong all the time.

Therefore, if communication problems seem to constantly arise between a leader and his staff members, the leader needs to take a good look at himself to see how he can improve the way he gives instructions. He should ask himself:

- Are my instructions clear so people can follow them?
- Would I understand my instructions if they were given to me?

- Are my thoughts complete so the staff can follow them all the way to a logical conclusion?

- Do my instructions leave people with unanswered questions, or do they feel like they have the necessary direction to accomplish the goal after I've finished speaking to them?

- After giving instructions, do I give the staff an opportunity to ask for clarification on points they may not have understood?

- Do I write down my instructions so staff members have a step-by-step vision before them of what I expect?

What if the majority of the team understands the leader's instructions 99% of the time, but one staff member keeps misunderstanding again and again? In that case, there must be something wrong in the way that particular staff member is listening. For some reason, he isn't hearing what others are able to clearly hear. Everyone else gets it, but he doesn't. It's obvious that this person has *a listening problem.*

Learning to listen is a skill that must be developed. If your head is so busy that you can't hear what is being communicated, you will miss important facts and details. In the end, your inability to listen will cause you to make mistakes in your assignment.

> If you don't slow down to really hear what your superior is saying to you, you will make mistakes that will lower his appraisal of you and your work.

If you want to please your superior, it's *essential* that you understand exactly what he wants. I guarantee if you don't slow down to really hear what your superior is saying to you, you will make mistakes that will lower his appraisal of you and your work.

LEARNING WHEN TO BE QUIET AND WHEN TO SPEAK

In James 1:19, the Bible says, "Wherefore, my beloved brethren, let every man be swift to hear, slow to speak, slow to wrath." The word "swift" in this verse is the Greek word *tachus*. It can be used to depict *a runner who runs as fast as he can so he can reach the finish line before his competitors.* Because this runner fiercely wants to win the race, he puts everything else out of his mind, focuses on the finish line, and then presses forward to obtain the first-place prize.

By using this word "swift," James is telling you that you should want to "place first" when it comes to listening! He is also telling you that it takes effort to really "hear" what other people are communicating to you.

Listening requires one to *focus* on what is being said. When I talk about listening, I'm referring to that moment when a person quiets his mind and shuts his mouth in order to *deliberately listen to* and *digest* what someone else is attempting to communicate to him. This is a challenge for anyone who has a busy mind and a lot of details in his life to think about.

> Listening requires one to focus on what is being said.

Take me, for example. If I don't make the choice to slow down and really *focus* on what someone is telling me, I know I will miss much of what he or she is trying to communicate. My mind is busy all the time.

I have a church to pastor, a ministry to oversee, and television programs to film. I go on ministry trips that take me all over the world. I am constantly writing books. Besides all that, I am a husband and father. I rarely have a moment when I don't have some important matter pressing heavily on my mind.

I've learned that I must discipline myself to listen to what people are saying to me. Otherwise, they'll think I'm listening when, in reality, I'm about a million miles away in my thoughts. Just because I'm looking into their eyes doesn't mean I'm really listening. If I'm going to hear what they're communicating, I have to push everything else out of my mind and deliberately *focus* on what they're saying. This is a matter of discipline that I've had to work at developing in my life.

If a person believes he has something important enough to say to me, the least I can do is give him the courtesy of listening. Even if I don't agree with what he's saying, nor want to do what he's asking, I should respect him enough to hear him out. To pretend I'm listening when I'm not is simply rude.

Through the years, I've had to train myself to be a listener. To make sure I've really heard the point being made to me, I often stop and repeat the conversation to the person speaking to me. I ask the person:

- Is this what you're trying to tell me?

- Is this the point you're making to me today?

- Is this what you want me to get from this conversation?

- Is this what you want me to do after we're done talking?

- Is this how I need to respond?

- Is there anything else I need to know about this?

If I've missed anything important in the conversation or misunderstood what that person was attempting to tell me, I discover it by asking these kinds of questions. At the same time, the person speaking to me is assured that he has had my complete and total attention. When my conversation with that person is finished, I should understand exactly what he was communicating because I *focused* on him and *listened* to what he was telling me.

Those who cultivate and develop the skill of listening make good team players because they're better able to understand other people's opinions and positions. These people have a good foundation for success because *listening is the first step of communication.*

> Those who cultivate and develop the skill of listening make good team players because they're better able to understand other people's opinions and positions.

However, learning to listen should begin early in life. As a parent, I continually work on helping my children develop their listening skills because I want them to succeed in their life pursuits.

Many times I've looked my children straight in the eyes and told them what I wanted them to hear, only to realize later that they didn't hear a word I said. They looked like they were listening. They looked right into my eyes. They were quiet while I was talking. But they didn't hear a word I communicated because their mind was somewhere else or because they were thinking about their next response to what I was saying to them. As a result, they missed the whole point.

Whenever this happens, I stop and take the time to go back to the beginning of the conversation and repeat it one more time. You see, I want my children to understand the value and importance of listening. Without that skill, they will make wrong conclusions, misunderstand instructions, and never reach their full potential in life. *Again, listening is the first step of communication.*

QUICK ASSUMPTIONS MEAN POOR COMMUNICATION

People are also prevented from really hearing what someone is telling them when they assume they already know what that person is trying to communicate. That kind of premature assumption guarantees that they won't correctly listen to what the other person is saying.

It is especially unwise to assume that you understand your supervisor's instructions. If you're smart, you'll do the following to make certain you know exactly what your leader is asking you to do:

- Take the time to ask questions.

- Make sure you understand what your supervisor wants you to do and when he wants you to do it.

- If you have any doubt at all about an aspect of the supervisor's instructions, don't take another step forward until you clear up all questions.

- If you leave a conversation with your supervisor pretending you understand when in reality you do not, you are responsible for any mistakes you make later because you didn't ask questions.

- Repeat back to your supervisor what he just said to you. Then if you misunderstood anything, he can clear up those areas of misunderstanding before you attempt to follow his instructions.

Believe me, your superior will be impressed when you ask him pinpointed questions to make sure you understand what he just said! And as you sum up your conversation with him, he will take note of how well you are able to repeat his instructions to him.

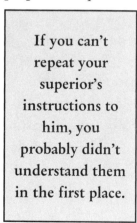

If you can't repeat your superior's instructions to him, you probably didn't understand them in the first place.

If you can't repeat your superior's instructions to him, you probably didn't understand them in the first place. So if there is something you don't understand, take the time to ask for clarification. Your superior will appreciate it, and it will save loads of time and mistakes later on down the road.

Besides, if you proceed with unresolved questions, you won't have the confidence to do the job well. You'll be harassed in your emotions, worrying that you might fail or do something wrong and end up being rebuked.

But there's no need to be bothered by these anxious feelings. Get rid of them by asking your superior for clarification. And when clarification is given, be sure you are listening with both ears and an open mind.

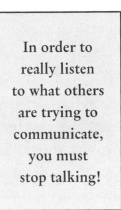

This is why James tells us to be "swift to hear." *Hearing is the foundation for all future actions.* You cannot appropriately act if you haven't understood what is being communicated. And you can't understand what is being communicated unless you have *listened.*

In order to really listen to what others are trying to communicate, you must stop talking!

A large part of staff communication problems can be summed up in this need to listen better. Therefore, a good team member will develop the art of listening when others speak.

It's Hard To Listen and Talk At the Same Time

James says that we should also be "slow to speak." The word "slow" is the word *bradus,* and it refers to *something that is slow or sluggish.*

In order to really listen to what others are trying to communicate, *you must stop talking!* You can't really listen and talk at the same time. That's a sure-fire way to miss important facts and details.

Sometimes when I speak to people, I can see that they're in such a hurry for their turn to respond or add their comments that they aren't really digesting what I'm trying to tell them. They need to learn how to slow down and stop being in such a hurry to answer. Then they'll be able to hear what is being communicated to them all the way to the end of the conversation.

When you withhold your comments and force yourself to listen to your pastor or supervisor, you are showing respect for him. The time for you to speak up or ask your questions is *after* he is finished talking. If you're afraid you won't remember what you wanted to say, have the foresight to take notes, jotting down your questions or comments. It will make you look smart when you refer to your notes while responding to your superior.

I'll give you another reason why it's good to be slow to speak up: If you wait just a few moments before you ask your question, it will probably get answered in the course of the conversation. One way to look really stupid in front of someone else is to make statements that reveal your ignorance. So save yourself from looking foolish in the eyes of others — refrain from inserting a lot of unnecessary questions or comments into the conversation.

Proverbs 18:13 says, "He that answereth a matter before he heareth it, it is folly and shame unto him." Learn to withhold your comments while others speak. Give yourself the opportunity to hear the entire matter before you respond. Slow your mind down. Discipline your emotions to be quiet. Keep your mouth closed while others are making their point. Then once you have fully heard what they have to say, *respond.* This is all a part of learning to listen and becoming a good communicator.

BEING A GOOD COMMUNICATOR IS
JUST AS IMPORTANT AS BEING ANOINTED

Learning how to communicate is just as important as being anointed when you preach. You may preach a good message, but if you can't effectively communicate with your followers, you'll never be able to build a church or an organization.

Only God knows how many powerful preachers have failed because they never developed their skill of effectively communicating to their followers. Anointed behind the pulpit, they were failures in one-on-one relationships.

When I look at the list of well-known preachers in the world, I see that most of them are skilled communicators. They know how to speak to people, communicate their heart, write a memo, and transfer what is in their heart into the hearts and minds of their followers. Because these ministers have cultivated this skill of effective communication, they are able to lead people forward into the future.

There are people in the world more gifted than those who are publicly recognized. However, because these gifted people don't know how to connect with others, their gifts and talents remain unknown.

It is my personal opinion that the greatest gifts in the world remain hidden from the public eye. Those who *are* well known are the ones who have mastered the skill of marketing, advertising, and communication. This ability to connect is what caused them to rise to the top.

This also applies to spiritual leadership. Perhaps a man has a pure heart, a solid revelation of God's Word, and a remarkable anointing. But if he doesn't know how to connect to the people under his authority, they will never truly follow him. His ability to deliver that anointed message from God's Word is determined by how well he links to the people under him.

Those serving under *you* should know the following:

- What your vision is.
- What is entailed in the job you want them to do.
- The standard of excellence you expect.
- The steps they should take next.
- The time frame for completing the task.
- The ramifications for a job not done on time.
- What the penalty is for a job done wrong.
- What the reward is for a job done faithfully.

To be a good communicator, you must make all these details clear so people can easily follow you. *Followers need* as *much information as you can give them.* You'll need to tell them again and again and again. Spell it out and make it as plain as it can be. If you want people to follow your instructions, make those instructions so clear that they *cannot* be misinterpreted.

If you don't know how to do this, you should do all you can to *learn* how to develop your skills of communication. Read some good books on the subject. Take a course in communication. Ask someone who is good at communicating to personally disciple you in this area of your life. If you'll develop this skill, you'll go far in your church or organization.

> If you want people to follow your instructions, make those instructions so clear that they cannot be misinterpreted.

But understand this: If you ignore this counsel and fail to learn how to communicate to your staff, workers, or followers, you are *chaining yourself* to a future of frustration. You are *confining yourself* to a small, unnoticeable church, business, or organization.

I thank God for the anointing. It empowers me as I preach. It strengthens me. It floods my mind with wondrous ideas that have powerful results. It inspires me and opens my eyes to divine revelation. It enables me to do what I could not naturally do. Without the anointing, I am *nothing*.

However, if I have the greatest anointing in the world but cannot connect with people to organize them into a cohesive unit pursuing a common vision, the world will *never* know about my anointing. My ministry will remain small and insignificant. Just a little adjustment in the way I relate to my staff and followers may make the difference between greatness or smallness, fame or obscurity, success or failure. This is true for *all* of us who serve in a leadership role.

DEVELOP YOUR OWN COMMUNICATION SKILLS

If you are a poor communicator, those who serve under you will always seem to be confused, not knowing what step to take next or what they should do. They won't understand your vision. They won't have a sense of direction. They will feel as though they have no plan to follow. They will lack a sense of accountability for their actions or decisions.

It's true that sometimes even when you do everything in your ability to communicate, some people just can't comprehend what you are saying. However, this shouldn't *always* be the case. So when this situation is repeated again and again, it should be like a neon light flashing in your face, alerting you that you are doing something wrong in the way you communicate.

Why did the apostle Paul write his letters? Because he wanted to communicate the revelation he had received from Jesus Christ.

Why did God send His Son into the world? Because He wanted to communicate His message of love to the world.

Why did the Holy Spirit inspire the writers of the Old Testament to write the Old Testament books? Because God wanted to communicate truth to His People.

- God is clear about sin.
- God is clear about the effects of sin.
- God is clear about the penalty of sin.
- God is clear about how to be delivered from sin.

- God is clear about how to be forgiven of sin.

- God is clear about hell.

- God is clear about heaven.

- God is clear about the Holy Spirit.

On issues of vital importance, the Bible is *absolutely clear.* God left no room for us to misinterpret what He says. It is possible to know exactly what God thinks about these central issues because His Word has vividly spelled it out for us. *The only reason we might not know what God thinks and expects is that we aren't listening.* God has made His thoughts on these key truths crystal clear.

- *If God is skilled at communication;*

- *If the apostle Paul was skilled at communication;*

- *If the Spirit of God is still communicating with us today;*

- *Don't you see that you also need to develop communication skills in your own life?*

This one thing can make the difference between your being a good leader or a bad leader. People won't judge you by your anointing — they'll judge you by the way you lead them. Communicate clearly, and they'll be yours forever. But if you communicate poorly, they won't stay with you very long.

TEST THE CANDIDATE'S COMMUNICATION SKILLS

So when you're choosing potential leadership, never ignore this issue of communication. If the person you're considering for a position cannot grasp the need for clear communication, he is *not* to be a leader. Even if his gifts and talents are enormous, don't use him until he first comes to recognize the vital importance of communication.

The prospective candidate's first test of communication must be between you and him. If he cannot communicate and be accountable to you in details you have requested, neither will he be a good communicator with those under him. *His communication with you must be the first test.*

In order to discover what kind of communicator that potential leader is, you must put him in a position in which he must *report* to you. Ask yourself:

- What kind of attention does he give to details?

- Does he skim the surface, or does he put some depth of thought into his reports?

- Does he give me the full picture, or does he carefully paint the picture he wants me to see?

Most people hate to fill out forms and give reports. Perhaps they don't like to deal with details, write letters, or keep track of seemingly mundane and unimportant information. *But a person's ability (or lack of ability) to keep you regularly and faithfully informed is a key to determining whether or not he is fit for leadership.*

> A person's ability (or lack of ability) to keep you regularly and faithfully informed is a key to determining whether or not he is fit for leadership.

Again, if a person cannot faithfully and correctly communicate with you, he isn't ready to be placed over a department or an area of responsibility in your church or ministry.

Don't immediately give the potential leader full authority in his area of ministry. Give him authority one step at a time. Once he has proven he is faithful on one level, move him up a notch to a higher level of responsibility. When he has again proven himself on that level, move him up again.

Promoting anyone *too quickly is* not wise. So to begin with, just give your prospective leader a little responsibility. Then observe what he does with it.

- How does he relate to and communicate with others?

- Does he seize power and manipulate those under his command?

- Does he lead by communicating needed information, or does he expect people to blindly follow his commands?

- Does he report to you any important facts, or does he neglect details that should be considered vital?

- Does he follow through on assignments, or does he drop the ball on matters too serious to neglect?

If the potential leader is going to be a good leader, he must *first* be accountable to you by giving you regular reports and updates. If he cannot provide *you* with the information you need or request, he will probably not provide good information for his followers either.

Information is *vital* in any organization. It clears up misunderstandings. It gives a solid footing to move into the future. *Giving followers knowledge helps them follow.*

Jumping off a cliff isn't comfortable for anyone. By giving followers knowledge and understanding, a leader makes it easier for them to follow him to their common goal. You see, most people will follow if they can see where they are going, why they are going there, how long it will take, how much cost is involved, and what the purpose of the venture is. That's why a good leader *must* communicate all those facts.

> By giving followers knowledge and understanding, a leader makes it easier for them to follow him to their common goal.

So before you put your final stamp of approval on a potential leader, *first* make sure he is skilled at communication. If he is not proficient in his communication skills, at least make sure he is willing to develop those skills.

Years of experience have taught me that when you promote someone too high too fast, everyone gets hurt in the end. *And if you bring a poor communicator into your leadership, you are opening the door for frustration to enter your ranks.*

So be careful and move slowly. Make sure you are selecting someone who will bring order to the ranks!

QUESTIONS FOR PERSONAL GROWTH OR GROUP DISCUSSION

1. What are some external signs of bad communication in a ministry or organization?

2. What are some of the elements of good listening?

3. What can you do to make sure you know exactly what your leader is asking you to do?

4. What steps can you take to make sure those under your authority understand your instructions?

5. What is the first important test of a potential leader's communication skills?

NOTES:

_____

_____

_____

_____

_____

_____

_____

_____

_____

_____

_____

_____

_____

_____

_____

_____

_____

_____

_____

_____

_____

_____

WHAT KIND OF HOME LIFE DOES THIS PROSPECTIVE LEADER HAVE?

I want to devote this chapter to a discussion about your potential leaders' private lives. In particular, I want to talk about their marriages, their children, the physical condition of the houses where they live, and the manner in which they manage their personal finances. These four points are extremely important when you're considering someone to be a part of your team.

I am fully aware that this discussion may raise more questions than it answers. This chapter is not intended to be a comprehensive look at the questions addressed. Rather, it's designed to emphasize the point that these questions need to be addressed. What happens in a person's private life affects his public ministry. This is why I always take a look at a potential leader's private life before I invite him or her to fill a top leadership position on my team.

Someone may argue, "But my private life and home life don't have anything to do with my ministry at the church or my ability to serve. You have no right to dig into my personal life!"

This way of thinking is wrong. *Public ministry begins in a person's private life.* What goes on behind closed doors in a potential leader's home will tell you *exactly* what kind of blessings or problems he or she will bring to your team. This is precisely why the apostle Paul *urged* Timothy to take a deeper look at potential leaders' family life before inviting them to be a part of his church leadership team (1 Timothy 3:4,5).

> **Public ministry begins in a person's private life.**

Think of it this way: Paul was letting Timothy know that the family life of potential leaders belongs on their "ministry resume." In other words, the on-the-job training of managing home life is extremely applicable to a person's readiness for promotion to public leadership. His or her spouse and children are excellent references. Even the condition of the family's home and personal finances gives valuable clues to the potential leader's readiness.

As we explore this facet of examining a candidate for leadership, remember that you're not looking to disqualify anyone; rather, you just want to determine a person's *readiness* for promotion.

You see, although every believer should be pressing toward the mark, what distinguishes potential leaders is that their heart and character have been transformed to the degree that others can follow after them. This is never more clearly revealed than in the home. God designed the home as a honing instrument for many of the qualities required in leadership, such as patience, loyalty, kindness, selflessness, faithfulness — and the list goes on and on.

It's also important to realize that you shouldn't be looking for perfection as you examine a potential leader's home life. As always, God is looking at a person's heart and character, and so should you. You should look not for a candidate free of problems, but for one who knows how to turn to God and manage life's challenges according to Scripture.

THE EFFECT OF A LEADER'S HOME LIFE
ON HIS PUBLIC LIFE

When I was a teenager, there was a pastor in our city who had served his church for many years. He was deeply loved by his congregation, but his home life was vexed with a constant onslaught of problems. His children were rebellious; his wife rarely attended church; and his finances had been wasted because of his children's ungodly behavior.

Church members would often talk in private about replacing this pastor with someone else. But they knew if they asked their pastor to resign, they would be dealing another severe blow to his soul, which was already tormented by this difficult predicament at home. Their pity for him superseded their respect for him as they observed the inconsistencies and errors that were evident in the way he managed his home.

Because the congregation was so aware of their pastor's personal struggles with his family, much of what he had to say was powerless and ineffective. He just didn't have a home life to back up his message. The words of his messages were right; however, his family life was so chaotic and his children so rebellious that people silently moaned when he touched on any subject having to do with family. To much of the congregation, this pastor's words seemed empty and irrelevant.

I remember hearing people say, "I love our pastor, but who is he to tell us how to deal with our children? *He can't even deal with his own children.* And how can he stand in that pulpit and scold us for not being faithful in our church attendance? *His own wife doesn't even come to church!*"

I know of countless examples like this that demonstrate the importance of a leader's private, personal life. If a leader has a life to back up his message, people will listen to him and respect his words. But if he tries to tell others to do what they know he isn't doing in his own personal life, he negates both his message and his authority to speak into their lives.

> If a leader has a life to back up his message, people will listen to and respect his words.

Never forget that when you're a leader, the most important pulpit you'll ever possess is the testimony of your own personal life.

Please don't suppose that I'm picking on pastors. Pastors are real people who must deal with devilish attacks in their families just like everyone else. Everyone has struggles to overcome — including pastors.

But whether you serve in a leadership capacity in a church, business, or organization, your influence is only as strong as your personal life. If your personal life is suffering and people know it, your influence over them has already deteriorated.

PEOPLE WANT LEADERS WHO
DEMONSTRATE THEIR MESSAGE

Most people who sit in the church pew have struggles of their own at home. They're praying and crying out to learn how to overcome their obstacles and difficulties. This is one reason why the personal life of a leader is so important. People need leaders who are out in front leading the way, showing them step-by-step how to live successfully during both the challenging and prosperous times of life.

In First Thessalonians 2:8, the apostle Paul gave a dynamic, life-changing principle that I've found to be very helpful in my own ministry. He wrote, "So being affectionately desirous of you, we were willing to have imparted unto you, not the gospel of God only, also our own souls, because ye were dear unto us."

Think about Paul just for a moment.

Paul was the crème-de-la-crème of New Testament theologians. He could have lectured for multiplied hours from the vast wealth of information and revelation stored up in his incredible intellect — and I'm sure that from time to time he did this. But Paul didn't just lecture and preach. He gave the people not only the Gospel, but also his own soul. His "soul" was his life, his emotions, his view of things, his lifestyle. He lived so openly before the Church that he was able to *model* his message before them.

This openness was evidently a part of his relationship with Timothy as well, because he told him, "But thou hast fully known my doctrine, manner of life, purpose, faith, long-suffering, charity, patience" (2 Timothy 3:10). The words "fully known" are from the Greek word *parakoloutheo*. It describes *a person who has followed someone else so closely, he is now able to duplicate the life and actions of the one he's been following.*

Paul's life was no secret to Timothy. It had been an open book to him. Timothy read Paul's life, studied his behavior, and possessed a knowledgeable insight into Paul's lifestyle. This is why Paul could say, "...thou hast fully known my manner of life...."

Timothy knew Paul's manner of life — *his lifestyle, his faith, his determinedness, his persistence to keep going and going regardless how difficult the task or assignment.* This gave Paul a right to speak into Timothy's life about "enduring hardness" (2 Timothy 2:3). Because Paul himself had been proven and was known to be a good soldier of Jesus Christ, Timothy knew Paul's message was valid. *Paul's life backed up what he said.*

Now look at Acts 20:33-35. Notice that before Paul told the Ephesian elders, "It is more blessed to give than to receive," he reminded them of his own example that he had lived before them:

> I have coveted no man's silver, or gold, or apparel. Yea, ye yourselves know, that these hands have ministered unto my necessities, and to them that were with me. I have shewed you all things, how that so labouring ye ought to support the weak, and

**to remember the words of the Lord Jesus, how he
said, It is more blessed to give than to receive.**

Everyone knew that Paul had worked to support his own
team. So when he urged the Ephesian elders to support the
weak, his message was not just a theoretical lesson. *It was backed
up by his own personal life.*

PEOPLE NEED AN EXAMPLE TO FOLLOW

The Bible stresses how important it is for leaders to serve as
godly examples for others to follow. Hebrews 13:7 says,
"Remember them which have the rule over you, who have
spoken unto you the word of God: *whose faith follow,
considering the end of their conversation.*"

What makes a leader's life such a powerful example is the
outcome or the end result produced by his own life and actions.
A person's message on faith makes a powerful impact on me
when I know this person has accomplished great things with his
faith. He isn't just speaking abstract theory — *he's speaking out
of his own life experience.*

Likewise, a person's teaching on finances and giving makes a
powerful impact on me when I know that person is personally a
giver and has seen God's miraculous provision in his own life
and ministry. He isn't just speaking abstract theory — *he's
speaking of his own life experience.*

When I hear someone teach about walking in covenant, I
want to know if this person is himself a man of covenant. If I
learn that he has walked in covenant with brothers in the Lord

for years and years and has paid a price to keep that covenant, his example impresses me so much that my heart is open to hear what he has to say. He isn't just speaking abstract theory — *he's speaking out of his own life experience.*

When someone teaches on church growth, I want to know how many churches he's pioneered and pastored. What kind of church growth did he personally experience? Is this just a theory he picked up in a book or seminar, or am I listening to someone who really knows? If I learn that this person has a life and testimony to back up what he's preaching, it opens my heart to hear what he has to say. Again, he isn't just speaking abstract theory — *he's speaking out of his own life experience.*

Nothing is more powerful than a message backed up by a life.

People are looking for someone who can *demonstrate* victory and success to them. People need an example. They need leaders to lead them, both by *their message* and by *their example,* because people want to know that this kind of victorious life is really attainable.

- If people see that their leader doesn't know the voice of God at least a little better than they do;

- If they see that their leader isn't willing to make the sacrifices he requests of his followers;

- If they see that their leader's family is out of order and filled with deep-seated problems;

- If they see that their leader and his spouse are in constant conflict with each other;

- If they see that their leader's home life is chaotic and turbulent;

- If they see that their leader's personal finances are messed up because of irresponsible actions;

- THEN they will not be inclined to follow the message or example of that leader.

And why should people follow someone who has demonstrated a lack of victory in his own personal life?

THE VITAL EXAMPLE OF A GOOD HOME LIFE

Especially in our world today, people need their leaders to provide good examples of successful home lives. One statistic reported by one of the world's largest statistical firms indicates that Christians are more prone to divorce than non-Christians.[1] This simply shows the extent to which the world and its ungodly influences have crept into the Church during these last days.

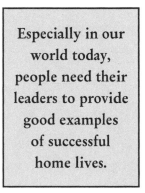

Especially in our world today, people need their leaders to provide good examples of successful home lives.

Marriages and families are under intense, demonic attack these days. This makes it even more crucial that people placed in leadership positions serve as godly examples in their home lives.

However, neither you nor I will ever find a perfect leader with a perfect marriage and perfect children. Every person deals with conflict on occasion in his marriage and home. So when I

---

[1] George Barna, *The Second Coming of the Church* (Nashville: Word Publishing, 1998), p. 6.

say people need leaders to be examples, I am emphatically *not* saying that leaders must be perfect — only that they must be "blameless."

What do I mean by "blameless"?

First of all, Paul is the one who wrote that leaders must be "blameless" (1 Timothy 3:2). This word "blameless" scares many of us because we think it means we must be perfect. But no one can be perfect, so we can stop worrying about that!

> Paul never expected anyone to be perfect this side of heaven.
> But he did expect his leaders to be "blameless."

Paul never expected anyone to be perfect this side of heaven. But he did expect his leaders to be "blameless."

The word "blameless" is the Greek word *anepilemptos*. It literally means *not able to be taken hold of.* It describes *a person who has no flaws in his character that might prove to be a stumbling block to people, hindering them from following him.*

The pastor I told you about earlier in this chapter is an example of a person who wasn't blameless. Because this pastor's family was out of order, *he lost his authority to speak to his congregation about issues of home, marriage, and family.*

If a person has made a mess of his own finances, his followers will not take him seriously when he speaks to them about being responsible with money. He has lost his authority to speak on this issue.

If a person has children who are out of control, his followers will not listen to him when he tries to lecture them about their own children. He has lost his authority to speak on this issue.

When a leader lacks credibility in his own personal life, he forfeits his authority to speak to others who are facing similar struggles. So when Paul says that a leader must be "blameless," he is giving us good, solid advice.

> When a leader lacks credibility in his own personal life, he forfeits his authority to speak to others who are facing similar struggles.

If you're going to choose someone to be a godly example to the flock, make sure that person is really *an example*! Be certain that nothing is so seriously wrong in the prospective candidate's life that it would eliminate his or her influence in people's lives.

AN EXAMPLE IN THE BASICS

When Paul wrote Timothy and gave him a list of requirements for spiritual leadership, he said a leader must be "one that ruleth well his own house, having his children in subjection with all gravity; (For if a man know not how to rule his own house, how shall he take care of the church of God?)" (1 Timothy 3:4,5).

This in no way implies that a person must be married and have children in order to hold a leadership position. Paul is simply stating that if a leader is married with children, that leader should possess these traits in his or her home.

However, the principle Paul lays out in this verse applies to the single leader too. The fact is, whether married or single, a leader's home life should demonstrate order and discipline — or, as Paul said, every leader should know how to "rule well his own house."

As I've considered these verses over the years, I've come to see four major areas that have to do with "ruling" one's household. In our own ministry, I've learned to pay attention to these four areas. I make it a point to explore how well a potential leader fares in these areas of concern before I put my final stamp of approval on him or her as a new team member.

> Every leader should know how to "rule well his own house."

I've learned that reams of information about potential leaders and how well they will serve in their new leadership capacity may be ascertained by delving into these four points. So let's briefly review these four critical areas of concern. Afterward, we'll discuss each point in greater detail to provide a fuller explanation.

1) THE HOME LIFE

Paul said a leader must be "one that ruleth well his own house." The word "house" includes *everything about a person's home life.* In the following pages, you'll see that one of the most strategic factors to consider when selecting new leaders is the condition of their marriage — *if* the potential leaders are married. What kind of relationship do they have with their spouse? Is it a supportive, healthy marriage, or one that is full of problems? The answer to this question may give you great insight into the pluses and minuses that come with new potential leaders.

2) THE CHILDREN

Paul said a leader must be one who has "children in sub-jection with all gravity." If potential candidates have children (which is certainly not a requirement for leadership), perhaps nothing gives you clearer insight into what kind of leaders they will be than the example of their own children. Although you can't make this a hard and fast rule, most often the children of potential leaders are a reflection of the kind of leadership those candidates are cur-rently exercising in their own home.

> Since people can impart only what they have in their private lives, I want to know what potential leaders have imparted to their own homes.

Since people can impart only what they have in their private lives, I want to know what potential leaders have imparted to their own homes. What is the visible fruit of their influence and leadership in their children's lives?

- Do the children speak respectfully to elders?

- Do they speak respectfully to each other?

- Do they understand authority and submission?

- Do the children do what they are told, or do they ignore their parents' instructions?

The answers to these simple, basic questions are important indicators to let you know how potential candidates are leading their own homes. If they're not leading their own homes with excellence, why would you imagine they could lead an entire division of the ministry with excellence?

That's why it's important to never overlook a potential leader's children. They will always be one of the clearest signals to alert you to the kind of leader this person will be.

3) THE HOUSE OR APARTMENT

Paul wrote that a leader must be one that "ruleth well his own house." As already stated above, the word "house" refers to everything connected to home life. Part of home life is the physical house where the family lives. Therefore, it's valid to ask:

- What kind of home does this potential leader have?

- Is it well kept and maintained?

- Is it needlessly neglected? Does it look like it's falling apart?

- Is the yard mowed so this candidate has a good testimony with his or her neighborhood?

What exactly did Paul mean when he said leaders must *rule well* their own homes? In the pages to come, we'll look at this word "rule" to see exactly what he was referring to. But one thing is for sure: If a potential leader can't decently take care of his own domain, you don't want to put him in charge of *your* domain. That's why this is such a serious question to consider when selecting someone for a prominent place of leadership in your church, ministry, or organization.

> If a potential leader can't decently take care of his own domain, you don't want to put him in charge of *your* domain.

4) The Finances

In regard to finances, the phrase "ruling well his own house" leads me to ask, *"How does this potential leader handle his money and the payment of monthly bills?"*

How a person handles money is very revealing. It tells a lot about his personal integrity, his character, and how he respects the rights of others. When a person doesn't regularly pay his bills on time, he inconveniences and upsets other people's financial plans. This failure to keep financial commitments often reflects a lack of respect for others' needs and rights.

It also may simply be a sign that this person is immature in his understanding of money management and responsibility. Or he may not do well at saying no to his fleshly lust for material things. A person's financial problems may also be an indicator that he's experiencing problems in his marriage as well. Or perhaps his life is unstable due to irregular work conditions.

No matter which of these factors may be the cause for a candidate's financial problems, they are all serious enough to require thoughtful consideration on your part. Does this person have the time, energy, or maturity to handle a position of greater responsibility in your church, ministry, or organization?

I realize that some people may think I sound condemning and that I'm intruding too deeply into questions of such a personal nature. But it is impossible to separate a person's public life from his private life. What happens in one spills over into the other.

As I said earlier, *what's in your personal life is exactly what you will bring into your public life.* If you have order and peace in your private life, it will give you a solid foundation for public ministry. But if you struggle with disorder, chaos, turmoil, confusion, upheaval, and anarchy in your private life, it will obviously affect your ability to carry on publicly as a leader.

What happens at home really *does* affect your ability to work, serve, and follow God's will for your life. This is true not only for you, but for every leader you will ever choose.

Now let's go back and cover each of these four points of a potential leader's home life more fully.

A SOUR MARRIAGE CAN AFFECT YOUR MINISTRY

One of the most heart-rending things I've seen through the years is this sad situation: A person is called by God into the ministry or some type of spiritual leadership, but he or she is married to someone who doesn't have the same heart or vision. An even worse scenario is when a God-called person has married someone who is actually combative and antagonistic toward the ministry. This often leads to a tumultuous, stormy situation that produces constant hurt, strife, and turbulence on the home front, severe enough to hinder anyone from accomplishing his or her God-assigned task.

Amos 3:3 says, "Can two walk together, except they be agreed?" When a lack of agreement exists between husband and wife, it makes it very difficult for them to walk together. This unfortunate situation has affected the lives of countless leaders who knew what they were called to do, but could never freely do it because of a lack of agreement between them and their spouses.

When Denise and I first entered full-time ministry many years ago, the church where I served had many associate pastors on staff to help with the growing needs of the congregation. The church had grown to such a size that it was impossible for the pastor to do it all by himself, so the pastoral staff was very large. The experience of serving on that staff made many lasting impressions on my life.

One thing that impacted me was observing how the troubles in one associate's marriage greatly limited his effectiveness in the ministry. I was impressed by this man because he had such an intense desire to do God's will. But his home was filled with disharmony, conflict, and constant contention, making him nearly *paralyzed* in his ability to follow God's voice.

Denise and I had just gotten married. We were deeply in love with each other. We were elated about serving God together for the rest of our lives as a husband-and-wife team. We worked together, prayed together, and served our growing part of the church ministry together as husband and wife.

Even when my work required me to be away from home for incredibly long hours and even days at a time, I felt Denise's full support and knew she was at home praying for me. Although she couldn't be with me all the time, her positive attitude of support made her a critical part of the team.

Rather than sit home and feel sorry for herself because I was away, Denise would immerse herself in prayer for me. By doing so, she spiritually kept herself involved in whatever I was doing even when we were miles apart. She also got involved in the ministry herself as she sought to meet needs in the lives of other people. This involvement in the ministry brought Denise personal fulfillment and a sense of being needed. She didn't feel empty, left out, or ignored when I had to shift my attention somewhere else or travel away from her. My wife knew that she and I were in the ministry *together*.

But the older associate pastor in this story didn't have such a home situation. His wife practically lived a separate life and never attended church functions with him. After working with this associate for several years, I could count on one hand how many times I had met his wife. I even had to strain to remember her name! No one on staff knew her. She was distant from everyone and appeared to want no relationship with anyone on staff.

This associate was a very hardworking man who believed in what God had called him to do. After a while, I began to feel sorry for him.

Night after night, week after week, month after month, and even year after year, this man did everything in the ministry by himself. He frequently looked as though something heavy was on his mind. Often he came to the office in the mornings looking disturbed. Sometimes he would disappear during the day because something critical had occurred at home and he had to go home "to take care of business." He made nonstop excuses to explain why his wife never attended any functions. It was apparent he was "covering up" for whatever was wrong at home.

Finally, one day I asked him, "Is there a reason we never see your wife?"

That day he opened his heart to me and told me about his problem. His wife resented the fact he was in the ministry —

and because of that deep-seated resentment, she refused to participate in the church or the ministry to any degree.

- This explained the heavy look on the man's face;
- The troubled countenance I saw in his eyes;
- The plagued look on his face when he came to work in the mornings;
- The nonstop excuses he made for the absence of his wife at key events;
- The reason he did everything by himself, day after day, month after month.

Regardless of how this problem started or how it should have been resolved, the fact was that the stress and strain in the associate's marital relationship impeded him from being the leader he needed to be.

You could argue that the couple should have gone for counseling — and they probably should have. *They needed help.* You could speculate that the wife was wrong for having a negative attitude — and this would probably be a correct evaluation. *Her attitude was terrible.*

You could also debate that the husband was in the wrong — and this would probably be accurate too. *The man certainly made mistakes that aggravated the situation.* The truth is, both spouses had done things that contributed to this dilemma.

The situation became so grave that it *crippled* the man's leadership and *handicapped* him in fulfilling his charge as a man of God. Turbulence on the home front raged so unrelentingly that he was constantly distracted. Considering what he had to deal with at home, it was a miracle he was able to pull off any measure of success in his division of the ministry.

Unfortunately, I've seen this same scenario repeated time and time again over the years in many places all over the world. Let me assure you again: *What happens in your private life affects the way you serve in a leadership capacity.*

> If the marital situation at home is difficult, a potential leader will feel like he or she is fighting the devil on both fronts — both at home and on the frontlines of ministry.

If the marital situation at home is difficult, a potential leader will feel like he or she is fighting the devil on both fronts — both at home and on the frontlines of ministry. That candidate will most likely feel:

- Hampered
- Handicapped
- Encumbered
- Hindered
- Impaired
- Burdened
- Bound
- Frustrated
- Confused
- Angered
- Restricted
- Repressed
- Disadvantaged
- Paralyzed

On the other hand, a healthy marriage relationship will cause potential leaders to feel like they have a partner who is behind them and supportive of what they're doing. Candidates who have the support of their spouse have already won a very important battle. They've won the battle of strife and division on the home front and have therefore established a unified team. These potential leaders will doubtless feel:

- Upheld
- Reinforced
- Supported
- Bolstered
- Assisted
- Endorsed
- Encouraged
- Strengthened
- Unfettered
- Unobstructed

As I said, I could give example after example of people who, although called by God, were held back because of a messy situation at home. So when you begin to look for leaders, *never forget* to look at the relationship between the husband and wife. Ask yourself:

- Does this potential leader have the full, unrestricted support of his or her spouse regarding the ministry?
- Is the spouse of the potential leader in agreement regarding this new promotion?

These are critical questions that should not be overlooked or ignored. If you disregard this issue and never explore the kind of relationship that exists between the potential leader and his or her spouse, you may come to deeply regret that you didn't take this question more seriously. The last thing you need is a member of your team who is dragged down, defeated, and suppressed because of problems back home.

Occasionally marriages become difficult or problematic *after* a person becomes a visible leader. Perhaps hidden disagreements and feelings that have been suppressed for many years finally surface as a result of the pressures and responsibilities of the new position. When this happens, it can put a severe strain on that leader's ability to function.

In such an event, that leader needs to be very open and honest with his or her pastor or direct supervisor. The pastor or supervisor will probably detect that something is wrong anyway, since stress and strain at home always affects one's performance on the job. The necessary actions to be taken should be worked out between the leader and the person in spiritual authority at that time. To comment further on this point would be out of order, as each situation is different and requires a unique course of action.

Occasionally potential leaders are married to unbelievers. In our church, this isn't a hindrance unless their unbelieving spouse is against their deep involvement in the work of the ministry. Presently, we have two women on our staff who are mightily gifted by God and effective in their ministries, but they are married to unsaved men.

I knew this was the situation when I asked these women to join our team. Therefore, it was very important for me to determine how the husbands felt about their wives' working on our church staff.

You see, it just isn't wise to invite a person to become a staff member who has a disagreeing and unsupportive spouse. In doing so, you're inviting problems into that marriage. The situation builds resentment between the spouses and is ultimately destructive to their marital relationship.

> It just isn't wise to invite a person to become a staff member who has a disagreeing and unsupportive spouse.

If I had sensed any hint of disagreement from these two women's unsaved husbands about their wives' joining our staff, I'd have put on the brakes and said, "Let's wait until their husbands get saved." But because the women's husbands were supportive, I didn't find this situation to be a conflict or problem that would prevent me from inviting the women to become a central part of our team. Neither did I find my decision to be in conflict with any doctrine of the Bible.

This is a choice I made for our own ministry. As the leadership of each church or ministry faces these unique and distinct questions, they must come to their own conclusions and do what they believe is right according to the Word and their conscience.

I've found that making a hard and fast rule about such situations is not usually wise because each situation is different and requires specific attention to determine what should be done. *What works in one case may not be right for the next case.*

GOOD AND BAD MARRIAGES ARE USUALLY DETERMINED BY COMMUNICATION

Most marriage problems are communication problems. The husband doesn't know how to communicate to his wife. The wife has things to say, but doesn't know how to communicate them to her husband. As a result, invisible walls of resentment and offense are erected. Finally, the marriage is reduced to two people who live

> If you bring a person into your leadership team who has problems in his or her marriage, it may mean the person you have chosen has difficulty with communication.

in the same house but have no real relationship. And the root of the predicament can be found in a breakdown of communication.

In Guideline Number Two, I said that the essence of leadership is *communication*. If you bring a person into your leadership team who has problems in his or her marriage, it may mean the person you have chosen has difficulty with communication.

Maybe the person has a difficult time articulating what he wants to say. Or perhaps his spouse has tried to communicate, but he has a hard time listening. Either way, it's a communication problem.

Counselors from all over the world will tell you that most marriage problems would be remedied if viable communication existed between the husband and wife. A couple's marital problems may center around a variety of issues — work schedules, money problems, the children, sexual hang-ups, etc. But the bottom line is almost always their inability to successfully communicate about these topics.

Since what is in a person's personal life is exactly what he or she will bring into your public ministry, it's strategically important for you to look at the marital relationships of all potential leaders. See what kind of communication exists between them and their spouse. If they can't communicate at home with the most important person in their lives, are you sure you want them to be placed over a whole division of the ministry? If their communication skills with their spouse are poor, what makes you think they'd be able to effectively communicate with an entire group of people placed under their authority? You need to ask yourself:

- Is this potential leader a good communicator?

- Is there healthy feedback between the candidate and his or her spouse?

- Do I see them talking about their thoughts, feelings, and convictions?

- Do they have an understanding of each other's dreams and visions?

- Do they act like a team, or do they act separately and independently of each other?

- Is the candidate's spouse always the last to discover important decisions, or does the candidate make a practice of affirming his or her spouse's importance by communicating vital details?

- Do the candidate's children have an understanding of what their mother or father is called to do?

- Do the candidate's children feel as if they have their parent's ear when they need to talk, or do they feel like they're the last item on his or her list of priorities?

- What kind of communication goes on in this potential leader's home?

Since leadership is communication, *do not overlook* this issue of how potential leaders communicate with their spouse. If they can't communicate well at home, they probably won't communicate well in their division of the ministry either.

So take a thoughtful look at how prospective candidates communicate at home because that's probably exactly what you'll get if you put them in charge of some aspect of your church, ministry, or organization. *I've seen this truth proven over and over again throughout the years.*

MARRIAGE IS NOT A LEADERSHIP REQUIREMENT

I've spoken a lot about married people in this chapter, but what about potential leaders who are not married? Can they also be used in top leadership positions in a church or ministry?

In First Timothy 3:2, Paul wrote that a leader must be the husband of one wife. Some have mistaken this to mean that a leader must be married. But Paul wasn't saying that marriage is a requirement to be a leader; he was saying that a leader must have only *one wife* if he *is* married. The meaning of this phrase "one wife" is a tricky question that must be understood in the context of the New Testament. However, this is a issue I will deal with later in an upcoming book.

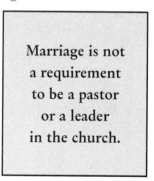

Marriage is not a requirement to be a pastor or a leader in the church.

The point I'm making here is that marriage is *not* a requirement to be a pastor or a leader in the church, although some leaders have tried to enforce this as a hard and fast law for leadership. If marriage were a requirement to be a spiritual leader, then many notable people in the New Testament were out of order and should have never been in the ministry.

For example, consider these single adult leaders in the New Testament:

- *John the Baptist:* There is no evidence to suggest he was married.

- *The apostle Paul:* He was definitely not married when he wrote his epistles.

- *Timothy:* There is no evidence he was married.

- *The apostle John:* There is no evidence he was married.

- *Jesus Himself:* Of course, Jesus wasn't married.

I'm amazed at how shallow some people swim regarding the way they arrive at their scriptural conclusions. With just a little deeper thinking and exploring of New Testament personalities, it becomes crystal clear that God isn't against using single adults in key leadership roles in the Church. In fact, Paul implies in First Corinthians 7:29-35 that single adults are freer to do the work of God because they're undistracted.

WHEN CONSIDERING A MARRIED PERSON TO BE A PART OF YOUR LEADERSHIP TEAM

When a prospective candidate is married, I recommend that you make sure the air is clear and everything is fully understood between both spouses. Bring both of them together for a talk before you seal the deal with that new leader. You see, even though you may have already asked the potential leader if his or her spouse is in agreement with the new promotion and added responsibility, you still don't know how well all the facts were communicated to the spouse.

If you need a married couple to be a part of your team, then love them enough to take the time to sit down, look them both in the face, and ask some penetrating questions. Verify that they really do agree on this issue of the candidate's accepting greater realms of authority and responsibility. Make certain that the new leader's spouse understands the situation by asking him or her:

- Do you understand the job I'm offering your spouse?

- Can you explain to me in your own words what your spouse's new responsibilities will be?

- Do you comprehend the hours this job will require in order for your spouse to fulfill his [or her] responsibilities according to my expectations?

- Are you willing to jump in and be a part of your spouse's new ministerial responsibilities?

- Do you have any hesitancy about this new development?

- Do you have any questions or fears that need to be cleared up before we get started?

- Have you and your spouse prayed and sought God's direction in this new development?

By asking potential leaders' spouses these questions, you have drawn them closer to the decision-making process and made them feel like they're just as important as the person they're married to. You've also provided one more opportunity to see how the couples respond to each other, to determine if they have harmony in their relationships, and to see how well the candidates have communicated the facts to their spouses.

CHILDREN'S BEHAVIOR TELLS THE REAL STORY ABOUT WHAT GOES ON BEHIND CLOSED DOORS

Once while traveling on an airplane, I sat next to a lady who had taught public school for thirty-five years. I asked her, "What can you tell about a family by the way a child behaves in school?"

She answered, "Everything! I can usually tell by the way a child acts if his or her home life is peaceful or tormented, if the parents pay attention to their kids or ignore them, and if the father and mother have a good relationship. Almost everything can be determined by watching a child's behavior. It's usually a mirror of what's happening at home."

Since that time I've asked the same question to Sunday school teachers and Christian school teachers all over the world. One after another, they all gave me the same answer: *A child mirrors what happens behind a family's closed doors.*

Of course, I know there are unique situations in which parents do everything right in raising their child, yet the child still becomes indifferent toward God and develops a rebellious and disrespectful attitude toward others. A precious family I know well comes to mind. The father and mother did everything they knew to do to be good parents and provide a loving environment for their children. Yet one of their sons rebelled anyway, creating chaos and disgrace for the entire family.

Sometimes this happens even when the parents have done everything possible to lead their child in the right direction. But notice that it didn't happen to every child in the family I just mentioned — *only to one child.* The other children were model children in every way.

So look to see if every child in a potential leader's family is troublesome, rebellious, and defiant. As that candidate's pastor or spiritual supervisor, you'd be foolish to overlook such a situation.

Rebellious children are a symptom of a deeper problem in the family. If only one of the candidate's children is rebellious and unmanageable, as in the case above, you might be able to dismiss the situation as a freak development or an attack of the devil. But if every child exhibits the same disturbing behavioral problems, you can surmise that something is not right in that home.

> When an entire family is plagued with problems, the root of these problems is usually found at the top.

Professional counselors will tell you that when an entire family is plagued with problems, the root of these problems is usually found at the top — *with the father and mother.* Something is usually wrong in the way they are providing leadership for their home. And if a potential leader doesn't provide proper leadership at home, you have no reason to assume he can provide proper leadership to an entire department of the church, business, or organization.

The apostle Paul said that a spiritual leader must have "children in subjection with all gravity." So when I choose leaders for my team, I'm always careful to take an observant look at their children. If this potential leader cannot successfully train and disciple his own children, I can't expect him to be able to do the same with adults. *Adults are much harder to deal with than children!*

I appreciate Paul's practical approach to leadership selection. He didn't overspiritualize this question. He just went straight to the bottom line, urging Timothy to check to see how well his potential leaders had done with their own kids. In Paul's view, if potential team members can't lead well at home with the kids, then they won't be able to lead well at church with the adults either: "For if a man know not how to rule his own house, how shall he take care of the church of God?" (1 Timothy 3:5).

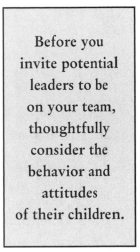

Before you invite potential leaders to be on your team, thoughtfully consider the behavior and attitudes of their children.

In our church and ministry, I learned that disrespectful children are usually an indicator of a serious problem in the home. At church, everyone may dress beautifully and smile just right. But if there is disrespect between parents and their children, it's usually (not always) a sign that the home is out of order.

So before you invite potential leaders to be on your team, thoughtfully consider the behavior and attitudes of their children (if they have children). I recommend that you observe their children and ask yourself:

- Do these children understand authority?

- Do these children demonstrate respect and honor for their elders?

- Do these children demonstrate respect and love for each other?

- Do these children talk disrespectfully to their parents?

- Do these children do what they're told to do?

- Do these children play one parent against the other parent — going to the second parent to get approval for what they want to do after the other parent has already denied their request?

- Do these children argue with their parents?

- Do these children understand their daily responsibilities around the house?

- Do these children have tasks at home that are their sole responsibility?

- Do these children attend church regularly?

- Do the parents have to beg and plead to get their children to obey them?

- Would I be proud of these children if they were mine?

The answers to these questions shouldn't be overlooked or ignored. Your answers won't determine how good or bad the children are. Rather, the answers will reveal how well or how poorly the parents have done in training and teaching their children.

Also, it's important to realize that some adults came to the Lord late in life; therefore, their children's lack of discipline or respect may have already been an established fact before the parents came to Christ. The parents may be trying to correct an out-of-order situation that developed during their old life before they got saved.

So check to see if the parents are taking the proper steps to bring order to their home. Although the situation may not be totally right yet, the fact that a potential leader and his or her spouse are serious about bringing their family under the Lordship of Jesus Christ is a good sign. As you watch to see how the couple begins to bring order into a disorderly situation, you'll discover what kind of "stick-to-it-ive-ness" they possess in regard to implementing godly decisions in their home. You may be impressed enough with the candidate's dedication to allow him or her to serve as a leader, even though the home situation isn't quite what it ought to be yet.

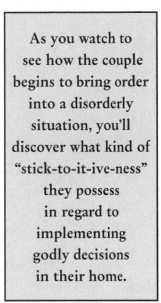

As you watch to see how the couple begins to bring order into a disorderly situation, you'll discover what kind of "stick-to-it-ive-ness" they possess in regard to implementing godly decisions in their home.

WHAT AGE CATEGORY OF CHILDREN IS PAUL TALKING ABOUT?

Paul wrote that a leader must have "...children in subjection with all gravity" (1 Timothy 3:4). Let's look at this word "children" for a moment to determine the age category the apostle Paul was referring to. The word "children" is the Greek word *tekna*. It is most widely used to describe *children who are still under parental guidance at home.*

Some years ago, I was present at an election for a Pentecostal Bishop in the former USSR. This man was superlative in his Christian life and testimony both before the church and the world. He was currently serving as Bishop and was up for reelection at that meeting. As it came time to cast votes, the leader of the vote asked, "Is there anyone here with a reason why this man cannot continue to serve as Bishop?"

A man stepped to the microphone and said, "Yes, I know of a reason that he can't serve as Bishop. His son isn't serving God. As a matter of fact, his son has a bad reputation in this entire community. This Bishop's house is not in order. Therefore, he should not be allowed to continue serving as Bishop."

I watched sadly as the Bishop stood to explain the situation. During the past year, his twenty-five-year-old son had strayed from the Lord and made some mistakes. The young man had already recommitted his life to Christ and was back in church again. But because of the mistakes he had recently made, the entire group of pastors debated back and forth about whether or not the Bishop should be allowed to continue to serve in his present position.

However, when Paul wrote that leaders' children must be in subjection, he was referring to children who are living at home and are still under parental guidance. At some point, those kids grow up and become responsible for their own spiritual lives. This verse obviously applies to leaders who have younger children still living at home — not to leaders whose children are grown up and have moved out on their own.

'IN SUBJECTION WITH ALL GRAVITY'

Paul said children must be "in subjection with all gravity." Let's look at these words "subjection" and "gravity" to determine what Paul was trying to communicate to us.

The word "subjection" is the Greek word *hupotasso*. It is a military term that was used to describe *being under command or under authority*. It is the picture of *a soldier who knows who his superior is; understands how to respond to that superior; and knows his own place, function, and assignment in the army.*

- A soldier knows how to speak to his commanding officer.

- A soldier knows what will happen if he speaks disrespectfully to his commanding officer.

- A soldier knows who is in authority over him and is taught to respect that authority — even if he doesn't agree with it or enjoy it.

A soldier also understands his daily responsibilities and assignments. For example, no soldier in the army, wakes up and says, "Gee, I wonder what they'll ask me to do today?" He knows that certain responsibilities are regular and routine. He understands that he is expected to fulfill these basic duties each day — duties such as:

- Making his bed.

- Combing his hair.

- Grooming his face.

- Shining his shoes.

- Wearing clothes that are pressed.

These responsibilities are not optional for the military soldier. He doesn't even have to think about whether or not he should do these things because he already knows they are absolutely expected of a soldier in basic training.

If a soldier fails at these basic duties, he knows *beforehand* that it will be viewed as disorder and disrespect. He knows *beforehand* that failure at this most basic level will result in some kind of penalty. These expectations and penalties for failure to comply are *known* to each and every soldier from the onset of basic training.

By using the word "subjection" (Greek, *hupotasso*), which embraces this picture of military order, Paul is telling us that children need to understand how to submit to and honor authority. He is also telling us that, like soldiers, children need daily discipline — including responsibilities that are required and expected of them each day. This kind of "basic training" helps children understand the realities of work, the responsibilities of life, and how to be a part of a team.

It is my personal view that it's *wrong* to let a child vegetate in front of the television or lay around with headphones

> It is my personal view that it's *wrong* to let a child vegetate in front of the television or lay around with headphones blaring music into his ears hour after hour each day.

blaring music into his ears hour after hour each day. I believe it's *wrong* for a parent to make a child's bed, clean up his room, pick up his mess after he showers, and wash his dishes after he eats. Yet so often the mother does what the child ought to be doing as a member of the family team. She makes the child's bed, washes his dishes, picks up his dirty socks, and vacuums the carpet all around his feet while he sits and watches television.

This kind of "schoolroom" represents an unreal picture of life for the child. In the real world, no one will do everything for him when he's an adult. He'll get a big shock when he goes out into the world and suddenly discovers that no one is going to be easy on him in the workplace and that he has to carry his own weight of responsibility.

What does a parent's "let me do everything for you" attitude produce in a child? It produces an approach to life that is thoughtless, inconsiderate, insensitive, discourteous, lethargic, self-consumed, self-indulgent, and nonproductive. This method of parenting may feel more comfortable to the children's flesh, but it teaches them nothing about participating in life. In this type of situation, who is at fault? *The parent or the child?*

Paul's use of the word "subjection" indicates that a child should be given responsibilities that he or she should regularly perform. That child should understand the rewards and penalties for not doing what is expected. All of this helps prepare the child for life.

In our home, when our children were younger, they were expected to do the following:

- Brush their teeth each morning.

- Take a shower and get cleaned up.

- Comb their hair and look nice.

- Make their beds and make their bedroom look orderly.

- Wash, dry, and put away the dishes.

- Help vacuum the carpets and sweep the floors.

- Empty the wastebaskets and take out the trash.

- Make minor household repairs if they saw something that needed to be fixed.

- Keep their bathroom clean and proper.

- Take their dirty clothes to the laundry room.

- Know how to press their clothes and keep them looking nice.

If our children failed at these basic responsibilities at home, they understood the ramifications. Everything expected of them was *known.* Every penalty for a lack of participation was also *known.*

As a result, our home was orderly, peaceful, and looked nice most of the time. Even more importantly, our children felt a sense of responsibility and value for what they contributed to the overall picture. They understood that they were a part of the family team.

As Denise and I taught our children responsibility at home, we prepared them for the workplace when they got older. As we helped them understand submission to authority, we taught them to honor and respect any future supervisor, boss, or pastor they would serve. And as we taught them to honor their role as a part of our family team, we were building a strong foundation in their lives to help them function as valuable team members in the future. As parents, Denise and I were responsible to impart all of these lessons to our children.

If a potential leader is satisfied to have children who contribute nothing to the family, do nothing around the house, and have no routine assignments or duties that are expected of them. I would strongly recommend that you don't put this candidate in a key position yet. Learning to oversee and delegate begins at home — and if potential leaders are failing to delegate at home with their own kids, it's doubtful that they'll be able to do any better with adults.

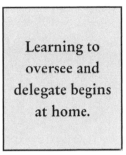

Learning to oversee and delegate begins at home.

How Do the Candidate's Children Speak to People?

Paul went on to say that a leader's children must be in "subjection with all gravity." Let's take a look at this word "gravity" to see what Paul was talking about. The word "gravity" is the Greek word *semnotes*. It presents the idea of *a person who carries himself with dignity and treats other people with courtesy and respect.*

Dignity

Look to see how the potential leader's children carry themselves. Do they appear to be children with a healthy dose of self-confidence, or do they seem to have a poor self-image?

I realize that parents are not 100% responsible for a child's perception of himself. However, it *is* the parents' responsibility to build a healthy self-image and confidence into their child.

Pay close attention if a child appears brow-beaten and downcast most of the time — especially if all the candidate's children seem this way. It may be a warning sign that this parent you're considering for leadership doesn't possess the necessary skills to build confidence in others.

If parents don't take the time to invest their lives and love into their child, it will usually be evident in the way that child carries himself. It isn't difficult to see if a child feels loved — just look at the way the child acts and responds to different situations. This will usually tell you how valuable the child feels in this world.

A good leader must be one who can build strength and confidence in other people. Everyone feels afraid to step out to do something new — so a leader must be able to impart enough confidence into people to take that next bold step of faith. If a potential leader has never developed the ability to do this with his own children, it's doubtful he will be able to do it with adults.

COURTESY

Courtesy is something that must be taught and developed. It shows care, sensitivity, and honor for other people. Knowing how to treat others with courtesy is essential in the life of a leader because he has to be so connected to people.

When I am considering potential leaders, I want to know how much they value this quality of treating others with courtesy.

Therefore, I frequently check to see if they have imparted that quality to their own children. If courtesy is important enough to cause them to teach and enforce it in the lives of their children, then I know it's a trait that they themselves value. So I look at a potential leader's children and ask:

- How do this potential leader's children speak to other adults?

- Do I sense that these children honor and respect those who are older than they are?

- How do these children address older people?

- Do these children serve themselves first, or do they let others go before them?

- How do these children treat people who are of a different skin color?

- Do these children interrupt other people when they are talking?

- Do these children monopolize every conversation, or do they make room for others to talk too?

- Do these children say, "Thank you" for deeds done on their behalf?

- How do these children act when they're in a boring situation?

- Do they speak to adults as though they were their equals?

Leadership is all about working with people, so the issue of courtesy is an important question. Knowing how to treat people is part of a responsible leader's job. Those who possess this quality are well-esteemed among their followers. On the other hand, those who show no courtesy for others are usually not well thought of.

So take a look at the children of your potential leaders. Make sure they have taught their children this important quality of courtesy.

RESPECT

Through the years, I've learned that the way a person's children speak to each other and to others outside the home is very revealing about what's really happening behind closed doors in that home. I'll say again that children usually mirror the true situation in a home. In other words, how they speak, carry themselves, and treat others usually reflects the quality of relationships in their home.

If parents are constantly arguing and screaming at each other until it has become a pattern and a way of life, that's usually exactly how the children will speak to each other in that home. When siblings engage in chronic patterns of strife, name-calling, and accusing each other, these destructive patterns probably exist between the parents as well. Children repeat what they see their parents do.

Not too long ago, I was called upon to mediate a very difficult situation between a husband and wife whose marital problems could no longer be hidden. On the surface, they always smiled and acted deeply in love. However, the behavior of their children let me know that serious problems existed in that marital relationship.

Those kids frequently told each other:

- "I hate you!"

- "I wish you were dead!"

- "I can't stand you!"

It was very revealing to me that children spoke so freely to each other like this and no one at home stopped it. It told me that it was probably the kind of language spoken by everyone in the home — *including Dad and Mom.*

Then the true story came to light, and the facade of marital bliss this couple tried to project was removed. The truth was that this husband and wife fought like cats and dogs. He yelled, and she screamed; he threatened, and she threw objects. That house had been filled with strife, discord, quarreling, and squabbling for many years. This sustained destructive behavior was exactly what those kids mirrored in their own behavior and conversations with each other.

When the truth came out, I wasn't surprised. Long before, I had told Denise that this couple had marital troubles, even though their facade seemed to project the opposite. The behavior of the kids gave away the truth of the matter.

> If a home is filled with love, respect, and teamwork, this is also evident in the way the children conduct themselves.

If a home is filled with love, respect, and teamwork, this is also evident in the way the children conduct themselves. For instance, just recently a leader and his family came to our home for dinner. I watched that leader's children interact with each other all evening while they were at our home. By watching those children, I knew exactly what I needed to know about this family. Those children possessed a respect and courtesy for each other and for other people that had been passed down to them by their parents' example.

Often if a potential leader has sour feelings toward authority, this will also usually be seen in the attitude that his or her children have toward authority. *What the parents feel and do in measure, the children feel and do in a greater measure.* So once again, just look at the children if you want to see what the truth really is about a potential leader.

When children are disrespectful toward authority and resentful when they're asked to do something they think is too low for them to do, it usually means that they come from a home where a servant mentality is nonexistent. If their parents were true servants, their children would reflect that servant mentality themselves. Leaders who are servants most often have children who are servants. So if you see a house full of children who are content to sit and watch other people work, be careful. You may be inviting someone who lacks a servant's heart into your team of leaders.

Never forget to take a good look at potential leaders' children. Although there are exceptions to the rule, you will most often find that what you see in the children is what you'll experience with the parent as well.

I am certain this discussion has raised questions I haven't answered for you. But my prayer is that it has raised a warning flag to make you think twice if you see a problem in a potential leader's children.

I'm not saying that a potential leader whose children are rude and disorderly can't be used. But you should enter that relationship with both eyes wide open. As we've discussed, the behavior of the children may be a warning sign of deeper problems in the parents' relationship with each other and in the way they relate to authority.

WOULD YOU WANT TO LIVE
IN THE CANDIDATE'S HOME OR ALLOW HIM
TO TAKE CARE OF YOUR HOME IN YOUR ABSENCE?

The apostle Paul said a leader must "rule well his own house." The word "rule" is the word *proestemi*. It means *to supervise; to oversee; to guide and direct.* The word "house" is the word *oikos.* It refers to *the overall concept of a home, including the house itself.* Paul is talking about supervising, overseeing, and taking care of one's physical home, in addition to taking care of the family.

> How a person treats his home usually reveals to you how he will treat your church, ministry, or organization.

How a person treats his home usually reveals to you how he will treat your church, ministry, or organization. The care of his home reveals his attention to details, his standard of excellence, the pride he has in the way he lives, and the high or low level of respect he has for himself.

I am so convinced of this that before I place someone in a top leadership position on our team, I pay a visit to his house —

unannounced. I don't want to give him an opportunity to clean up before I get there. I want to surprise him and see the true condition of that home.

If I knock on the door and the family is happy to see me, I already know they probably have a home that's in order. But if I knock on the door and they look shocked and dismayed, it usually means they live in disorder and don't want me to see the condition of their home.

If the dishes in the sink are piled two feet high, I know that the accumulation of dishes didn't begin that day. Those dishes have been sitting there for a while. If the wallpaper is peeling off the walls or the carpet smells like dog or cat urine, I know that this potential leader and I are not made of the same stuff. I could *never* tolerate that in my ministry.

If so many magazines, newspapers, and pieces of unopened mail are lying on the coffee table that there's no room to set down a cup of coffee when one is offered to me, I know that this person and I aren't compatible to work on the same team together. First of all, when I see all that old, unopened mail sitting there, I know that this person isn't up-to-date with important facts and details about his own life. Therefore, why should I think he would treat my ministry any differently?

On occasion I haven't been able to visit a potential leader's home, so instead I ask him to give me a ride across town in his car. This is just as revealing as visiting his home or apartment. If I'm covered with dog or cat hair when I get out of the car, I know there is a vast difference between this person and me. I would never be content to drive around for weeks in a car so dirty. If the car dashboard is covered with dust or the back seat is filled with trash — and it seems he's content to think this is a normal way to live — I know our styles are too different to be on the same team together.

By no means does God command us to live in a mansion or to drive a Mercedes. However, we should expect our leaders and ourselves to live in decent conditions. If potential leaders are satisfied to live like pigs at home, that's probably what 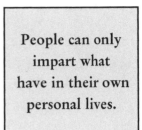 they will impart to their division of the ministry. Remember, *people can only impart what they have in their own personal lives.* If they don't have a needed quality at home, they probably can't give it to the ministry either.

Recently Denise and I had to be away from our home for a period of time. We discussed who should stay in our home during our absence. I suggested one particular person, and Denise said, "There's no way I'd let that person live in our house. It would look like a pigpen when we got home!" Denise mentioned another person, but I found myself saying, "That person is sweet but doesn't know a thing about responsibility. I'd be worried that she might burn the house down!"

As we talked, I noticed that all those we rejected as possibilities were people with whom we'd experienced trouble in their work at the church. These people love God and the church, and they love Denise and me. But they have no order in their private lives — and this disorder can first of all be detected in the low-level conditions in which they live at home.

Sweet as people like this may be, they are not compatible with me in a work situation because we come from two different worlds of expectation. I know that if I invite them to work with me, I'll have to deal with the disorder and mess they will bring with them.

So don't ask this type of person to be a part of your team unless you're willing to put up with his disorder and to work hard to bring correction into this area of his life. Certainly he needs correction and help, but you need to decide if you want to bring it to him while he's on your team or before he joins your team. Only you can answer that question.

DO YOUR POTENTIAL LEADERS PAY THEIR BILLS?

Another aspect of "ruling well one's own house" to consider is whether or not your potential leaders pay their bills and take care of their financial responsibilities.

When Denise and I first got married, I didn't have any sense of responsibility regarding money or paying bills on time. In fact, I knew it was time to pay the electric bill only when the electric company turned off the electricity! It wasn't that I didn't care. I was just young and didn't understand the importance of regularly paying bills. *Someone had to teach me.*

Then God put me under a pastor who believed in the gift of God he saw in me. This pastor took it upon himself to discipline me and help me eliminate this flaw from my life. He knew I wasn't trying to be irresponsible. I had just never been in this situation before — and it exposed an area of my life that needed to change.

If that pastor had never taught and corrected me, God wouldn't have entrusted to me the large amounts of money He has provided for our ministry over the years. I had to get my sense of personal financial responsibility straight if I wanted God to hook up with me in a big financial way for my ministry.

But what if a person repeatedly handles money wrongly? What if he has a strong desire to serve the Lord in the ministry but consistently doesn't pay his bills on time, nor does he even seem to care? Should you dismiss this as his "Achilles' heel" and just forget about it?

Money is a big test in life. Jesus said more about money than He said about anything else. How well a person handles his finances reveals:

- His understanding of responsibility.
- His attention to important facts and details.
- His concern about inconveniencing other people.
- His commitment to keep his word and the promises he has made to others.
- His concern about the kind of testimony he has before the church and the world.

It may be that this potential leader is as ignorant as I was when I first got married. Perhaps he just needs someone to jump into the middle of things and teach him how to do right.

However, helping someone in this way is an involved and lengthy process, so you need to ask yourself if you have the time to do it. And if you do have the time, do you also have the willingness to get that involved in this potential leader's life?

Someone needs to do it, but should it be you? Is it time for him to be a part of your top leadership team — or should you wait until this situation has improved? Only you can answer these questions.

If a potential leader is known to be irresponsible with money, it will be difficult for people to follow him. And if he's strapped with mountains of debt, you need to realize that he may have moments when he is distracted because of this heavy burden. That doesn't necessarily mean you can't use him, but it's important to seriously consider these factors before giving him a position on your leadership team.

ALWAYS ALLOW ROOM FOR MERCY

You're never going to find a perfect person. In fact, if these same questions were applied to you, you might not pass everything with flying colors either. So never forget to let mercy triumph over judgment.

> If your peace is disturbed because of things you see occurring in a potential leader's life, don't ignore what is bothering you.

But if your peace is disturbed because of things you see occurring in a potential leader's life, don't ignore what is bothering you. Pay attention to what your spirit is telling you. Perhaps he or she is the right leader, but it isn't the right time yet. It's better to be slow and sure than to move forward without the inner conviction that you're on the right track.

I pray this chapter has helped expand your thinking and broaden the scope of your considerations before you make your final choices for your leadership team. The Holy Spirit may give you greater insights than are written here regarding a candidate's home life. Just be open to let Him teach you how to distinguish between those who are and those who are not ready for spiritual promotion.

QUESTIONS FOR PERSONAL GROWTH OR GROUP DISCUSSION

1. Why is it important for you to live your life openly before those who are under you? Do you presently have an area of your home life that is out of order and would therefore serve as a bad example to others?

2. What happens if a leader lacks credibility in his own personal example regarding a certain area of his life?

3. What are some of the negative effects that a sour marriage could have on a prospective candidate's ability to lead?

4. How do you make sure that the spouse of a married person joining your leadership team is in agreement with this new situation?

5. In what way do children reflect the character and behavior of their parents?

NOTES:

_____

_____

_____

_____

_____

_____

_____

_____

_____

_____

_____

_____

_____

_____

_____

_____

_____

_____

_____

_____

_____

GUIDELINE NUMBER FOUR

HOW DOES THE CANDIDATE RESPOND TO CHANGE?

*L*et me speak to you about the challenge of dealing with changes and transitions that occur as your ministry or organization begins to grow and expand. Please stay with me clear to the end, as I intend to use many personal illustrations to demonstrate the point I want to communicate to you in this chapter.

If you want your church or ministry to keep growing and expanding, it isn't possible to keep things "the way they always were." I realize that it's a sweet and exciting time when you're just getting started in a church or organization. However, you can't stay at that same beginning level forever if you intend to have an impact.

For instance, in 1991 when we first started *Rick Renner Ministries* in the former USSR, it was an exciting time for all of us.

The vision was exploding in our hearts. Our small staff was not only committed to the vision, but we felt such camaraderie among us. We were like a little family.

I remember many times when I'd come into the offices in those early days and see our staff members holding hands and praying together, asking God for breakthroughs in the realm of television. We were in one accord practically all the time.

But as the ministry began to grow and be blessed by God, the workplace began to change too. We became busier. Because God was blessing, we didn't have time to just sit around and hold hands in prayer all day long. Our prayers were being answered, and now it was time to get to work. Believe me, we had loads of work to do!

From time to time, I heard staff members say, "You know, it just isn't like it used to be." But that's what happens when a church, ministry, or organization begins to be blessed with growth. Growth is demanding — and one of its demands is that everyone involved is able to accept and cope with *change*.

Some organizations are addicted to past memories and therefore can't reach into the future for what God has for them. They cling to "how things used to be" so tightly that they can't see how God wants things to be right now. This inability to let go of the past keeps them from grabbing hold of what God has for them in the future.

Let me assure you, holding tightly to past methods and ways of doing things is not the way to grow or develop. It stunts your growth. Of course, you must thank God for good beginnings and sweet memories. Those memories and experiences are foundational to what God has for you in the future. They're the very reason you *have a* promising future ahead of you right now.

But if you're so emotionally caught up in the "way it used to be" that you can't see how God wants it to be now, He may have to pass the baton from you to someone else. He is looking for someone who is willing to get up, get moving, and do what He wants done. You can't experience what God wants to do today while you're still clinging to the past.

MOTIVATING PEOPLE TO CHANGE

Motivating people to move forward into the future is a challenge for every leader. I know that from personal experience.

God has given Denise and me an extraordinary team to work alongside of us. We've been together for many years. Over and over again, our team members have demonstrated their willingness to follow my leadership.

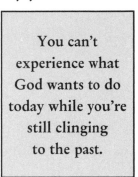

You can't experience what God wants to do today while you're still clinging to the past.

Through the years, the Lord has also given me many new and exciting assignments. I'm sure one reason He chose me is that He knew I would enjoy all those changes and new steps of faith. It's a part of my character to eagerly accept new, exciting challenges. In fact, receiving a new assignment from heaven really makes my heart sing!

My team has always had a heart to follow me through every change that has taken us into a new stage of ministry. One reason is that they *trust* me. They've watched me carefully and worked closely at my side through the years. They know I carefully think through my decisions and actions before I implement them.

People who can trust their leader find it easier to follow him. When I see how some leaders make rash decisions, changing their mind back and forth, it's no surprise to me that their team has a difficult time following them.

That's why I endeavor to provide a reliable atmosphere for my team. I let them know that I genuinely care about how my decisions affect them. My efforts along this line have helped build a strong foundation of trust between my staff members and me.

A STANDARD MUST BE ESTABLISHED
BETWEEN A LEADER AND HIS TEAM

As a spiritual leader, your life is your pulpit. In other words, you are to live your life as a godly example for others to follow. If you don't set a righteous example, it won't matter how hard you try to convince people to follow you — they'll still be negatively affected by what they see in your life.

It's tough for anyone to follow another person. It's even tougher when people are supposed to follow someone they don't trust. So if you're the leader, make sure your team members can safely place their confidence in you.

- They need to have confidence that you're careful in the way you make your decisions.

- They need to have faith that you really do hear the voice of God.

- They need to place stock in your credibility and believability.

- They need to feel secure in the knowledge that you're thinking about how your decisions will affect them.

- They need the assurance that you know how to make right choices and that you won't change your mind again and again.

Sometimes people are hesitant to accept change because of imaginary and unfounded fears. Other times the reasons for their hesitancy may actually be based in legitimate concerns.

For instance, leaders sometimes do things that make it more difficult for people to follow them. But if leaders expect people to follow them unreservedly, they should do everything in their power to make that process easier.

Some leaders announce all sorts of radical changes but never seem to follow through on them. In that case, the leader's team members may view his announcement of another new change as another grand plan that he'll start but never finish. This type of leader has crippled his own leadership by acting inconsistent and erratic in the way he makes decisions.

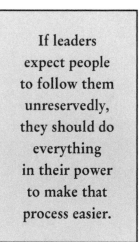

If leaders expect people to follow them unreservedly, they should do everything in their power to make that process easier.

So make sure you don't constantly tell your staff members, "The Lord told me to do this" or "The Lord told me to do that" and then never follow through on what you believe the Lord told you to do. If you make that mistake, you will hinder the ability of your team members to believe you. Your perpetual vacillation from one project to the next will destroy their confidence in your ability to hear from God.

When a leader is guilty of chronic vacillation between projects and of never finishing one project before starting a new one, it should be no shock to him when his leadership team shuns the thought of another new idea. They don't believe that leader anymore! He's announced too many plans that he didn't fulfill.

Now when he announces a new direction for his church or ministry, his staff members quietly surmise, "Yeah, we've heard this before! Let's wait and see how long this one lasts."

The apostle Paul told Timothy, "But thou hast fully known my doctrine, manner of life, purpose, faith, longsuffering, charity, patience, persecutions, afflictions, which came unto me at Antioch, at Iconium, at Lystra; what persecutions I endured: but out of them all the Lord delivered me" (2 Timothy 3:10,11).

Paul's manner of life gave him a platform of power and authority from which he could speak into Timothy's life. Timothy knew of Paul's consistency, faith, and endurance, so the younger man knew he was listening to godly, stable advice.

I can truthfully say that my leadership team knows my life too. They know I care about them. They know I don't quickly jump from one project to the next without prayer and seriously considering every aspect of my decisions. And they know I'll do whatever God asks me to do.

Yet even with this testimony of my life before my staff members, I have taken note that when I enthusiastically announce a new development in our ministry, they still need time to adjust and ask questions. This isn't a sign of rebellion. It's just a symptom of human nature. It's difficult for people to make the necessary adjustments for an upcoming change.

Time and again my team members have said to me, "Brother Rick, we're with you and we'll support you 100% of the way." But in my heart, I know the change I've proposed is difficult for some of my team members to accept — not because they're dragging their feet, but because they need a sense of security as I lead them into the future.

If I am to be a good leader, I have to realize that my decisions affect many other people's lives. What I decide for our ministry affects everyone who works for our ministry.

People naturally want to know:

- How will this change affect their job?
- Do they get to keep their same desk?
- Will they have to change offices?
- How will this change affect their work hours?
- Will they have to report to someone new, or will they have the same boss?
- Does this change mean they'll have a new chain of authority?
- How does this change affect everything they've done in the past? Is their past work still valid, or does this change mean everything they've done in the past is for nothing?

- Does this change put stress on the financial security of the organization?

- How will this change affect their families?

- Will they be able to emotionally handle all the changes that are going to be required of them during this transition?

If you were in your team members' position, you'd probably ask some of these very same questions. It's natural to ask these types of questions when those in authority over you announce a change that will affect a part or all of the ministry or organization.

Take time to reassure your staff members of your confidence that this change is proper and right. This assurance from you is essential so those under your authority can have a sense of peace and security as your ministry or organization moves forward. It's also essential that you live a consistent life before them because your life backs up any message you speak to your staff.

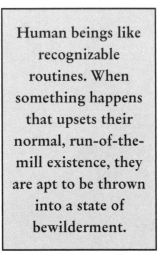

Human beings like recognizable routines. When something happens that upsets their normal, run-of-the-mill existence, they are apt to be thrown into a state of bewilderment.

Passing from one stage of development to another is simply a part of an organization's normal growth. Advancement to higher levels cannot occur without through transitions along the way.

Even so, dealing with change is one of the troublesome aspects of life that people face. Human beings like recognizable routines. They like to feel comfortable in their surroundings.

When something happens that upsets their normal, run-of-the-mill existence, they are apt to be thrown into a state of bewilderment. Even small changes that affect people's regular "routines" can be difficult for them to face.

ADJUSTING TO CHANGE AS NEWLYWEDS

When Denise and I first got married, I slept on the left side of the bed every night. But after a while, I got tired of sleeping on my left side and decided to switch sides for a couple of nights.

While Denise was in the bathroom taking off her makeup, I moved over to the right side of the bed. When Denise came to bed, she looked at me in shock and asked, "Why are you on *my* side of the bed?"

"I'm tired of sleeping on the left side of the bed every night," I told her.

I still remember her shocked response: "You can't do that! You're sleeping on *my* side. You're not supposed to change sides!"

I laughed and laughed as I rolled back to "my" side of the bed. I hadn't known until that moment how strongly Denise had taken possession of *her side*!

Denise's reaction to switching sides of the bed is a good example of the way people frequently view change. Rather than accepting change with enthusiasm, they see it as a disruption.

The truth is, change without purpose usually *is* a disruption. It's also often a sign of instability. It's true that sometimes people need to get shaken up a little bit to keep the dust of complacency from settling on them. But a leader who constantly initiates changes *just* for the sake of a good shaking makes it hard on his team members emotionally. This type of situation creates a disruptive atmosphere where things never have time to get set in place long enough to start producing real growth.

> I find change refreshing and invigorating *if* I know that it's from the Lord and will take me to a higher level.

Personally, I find change refreshing and invigorating *if* I know that it's from the Lord and will take me to a higher level. When I know there's a reason for change, I can embrace it with all my heart without a problem.

What if You Have a Person Who Refuses To Accept Change?

From time to time, every organization has a person who simply can't seem to get in the flow and embrace a needed change. This doesn't mean the resistant person is bad. The change being implemented has simply revealed his level of adaptability to a new situation.

If this person has served faithfully in the past, perhaps he can be repositioned in your organization to take on a different job — something he can do well despite his inability to wholeheartedly follow the changes you're trying to implement. After a little time, he may experience a real change of heart and come to understand the need for the change he once opposed.

Don't assume you have to fire a good person who has a faithful track record simply because he doesn't have the ability to see where you're leading right now. Give him time to adapt and to realize that your decision was right. The need for this type of managerial adjustment from time to time is just a natural result of growth.

But what do you do if, in the process of growing, you have to deal with someone who stubbornly resists and adamantly refuses to make the changes everyone else is willing to make? In this situation, you may be required to take a different course of action.

It's one thing for a person to experience difficulty when adjusting to change. But it's another matter altogether when a person puts out a rebellious stench so putrid that it affects the entire organization. If you have a potential or current leader who rebels against your authority and is mutinous in his attitude, you

> **What do you do if in the process of growing, you have to deal with someone who stubbornly resists and adamantly refuses to make the changes everyone else is willing to make?**

may have to remove that individual and replace him with someone who is willing to adjust to change.

You see, whenever ONE PERSON in your church, ministry, or organization believes his rights are more important than the overall plan or vision, he is no longer a benefit to the organization.

As much as you may love this problem person, you will begin to feel like you have a noose around your neck. The longer the situation lingers, the worse it will get. That noose of strife and rebellion will get tighter and tighter until it begins to choke the life out of your church or organization.

In the end, you'll feel like you're walking around on eggshells to avoid another conflict. Your focus will be more on "what he's going to be like today" than on the job you need to be doing.

A person who holds a church, ministry, or organization hostage by his wrong attitude in this way is displaying the ultimate in *selfishness*. If he is demonstrating this bullheadedness just to prove a point, he is grossly wrong. This situation reveals a very deep character problem in the person and a total lack of understanding about submission to authority.

If that person doesn't like or refuses to get in agreement with the direction the pastor or director is leading the church or organization, it would be far better for him to resign from his position than to constantly create an invisible barrier that everyone can sense.

When work relationships first begin, these kinds of character defects are not usually obvious. *But time is a great revealer of the truth.* Over a period of time, you will discover many characteristics about your current leaders, your potential leaders, and even about yourself.

If you have a person in your organization who is resistant to change, *take time to work with him.* Be honest and confront him about what needs to change in his attitude. *But if he still isn't able to follow, you will need to find someone else to lead. It has become a dead-end relationship.*

A NON-GROWING CHURCH

If your church, ministry, or organization doesn't have to deal with the challenges of growth, it is a signal that something is drastically wrong.

When Denise and I first started traveling and teaching the Word of God many years ago, I held meetings every year at a little church in the deep South that was filled with the sweetest people. This congregation displayed a southern charm and a level of warm hospitality that was just wonderful. But I knew there was something wrong with that church because year after year, it stayed exactly the same.

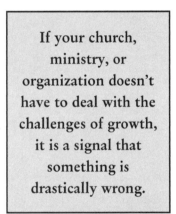

> **If your church, ministry, or organization doesn't have to deal with the challenges of growth, it is a signal that something is drastically wrong.**

When a church or ministry demonstrates no growth over a long period of time, it's a sure sign that something is inherently defective. The apostle Paul said the message of the Gospel produces "fruit" all over the world (Colossians 1:6). Part of that fruit is *numerical* as well as *spiritual* growth.

If a church or ministry remains the same year after year — the same message, the same people, the same music, the same children, and few newcomers — then the leadership needs to take a good look at what is being preached and promoted. When the Gospel is preached, it produces life-changing results and brings new souls into the Kingdom of God. *A healthy church, ministry, or organization always deals with challenges of growth.*

For years, I was puzzled about why this church never grew. They had a nice building, great teaching, and beautiful facilities for their children's ministry. I just couldn't figure it out.

> A healthy church, ministry, or organization always deals with challenges of growth.

Then one day the pastor opened his heart to me. He said, "Rick, on one hand, these are the sweetest people in the world. But on the other hand, they are so resistant to change, I can't implement one new thing in this church. If you only knew the argumentative spirit and opposition I deal with every time I want to lead the congregation forward. It's just shocking how difficult these sweet people can be!"

The congregation wanted everything to stay small and comfortably familiar, the way it had always been. In the end, God raised up another church on the other side of town to reach that city. Eventually that sweet little church Denise and I loved so much lost its joy and the precious fellowship they'd known and finally became divided by strife.

God wanted to use that congregation. He even gave them a pastor with a vision to lead them into the future. But because they refused to make necessary adjustments and embrace needed change, God's Spirit chose to use another church across town to reach that city.

FIVE POINTS TO PONDER IF A CHURCH
SHOWS NO GROWTH

If a church or ministry demonstrates no significant progress or numerical growth over a period of time, it's time to sit down and make an accurate assessment of the situation. Why isn't it growing?

A lack of growth is an indicator that something's wrong. Either the leadership is wrong in the way they're leading, or the team members are wrong in the way they're following. Either way, something is radically wrong when a church, ministry, or organization never grows.

If this scenario describes your church, ministry, or organization, I want to offer these five simple points for you to consider. These points will help you evaluate your situation so you can hopefully make corrections that produce change and growth.

1) REMEMBER

First, go back to the original vision God gave you for your church, ministry, or organization. Proverbs 29:18 says, "Where there is no vision, the people perish...."

When you stray from the original vision God gave you, it causes you to wander aimlessly. As a result, you begin to feel powerless and unproductive.

That's why its time for you to remember and reflect on the vision God first put in your heart.

Have you stayed in line with the original vision God gave you for your ministry? Have you deviated from that plan to go another direction?

Habbakuk 2:2 tells us, "...Write the vision, and make it plain upon tables, that he may run that readeth it."

When I sense that our ministry has become stagnant in any department, I go back to the vision God gave me for that part of our ministry. I refresh my memory. And with that vision now before me, I proceed to make a thoughtful review of the facts.

2) REVIEW

In the same way, it's time for you to *review* your performance in fulfilling that vision God gave *you*. Even if your church, ministry, or organization is growing and making progress, it's healthy for you to take the time to honestly look at what you have and have not accomplished.

Although the apostle Paul accomplished more than anyone else in his day, he wasn't satisfied with just knowing he was ahead of the rest of the gang. He took time to review the facts of what he had and hadn't accomplished. After reviewing the facts, he wrote, "Brethren, I count not myself to have apprehended..." (Philippians 3:13).

It's wise to review your current status. It's also smart for you to review the progress of your fellow workers and team members as well. See if they're on track or falling behind in the vision God gave you for your church, ministry, or organization.

Proverbs 24:3 (*TLB*) says, "Any enterprise is built by wise planning, becomes strong through common sense, and profits wonderfully by keeping abreast of the facts."

When you keep abreast of the facts, you know exactly where you are in terms of growth and progress. Staying ignorant of the facts is the fastest way to lose significant territory and to let another take your place of leadership.

> **When you keep abreast of the facts, you know exactly where you are in terms of growth and progress.**

3) REPORT

Once you've reviewed the facts, you need to make an honest analysis of your situation. It's time for you to make a *report* about your situation.

That's what my top leadership and I do after we've conducted an honest review of what we're doing well and what we could do better. We stop to talk about it. *We make a report.*

It's essential that we take the time to recount the facts to each other. This brings the harsh truth of reality to the forefront where it cannot be ignored or denied. Once everything is out on the table for all of us to see, we must make a choice:

- We can sweep the problems under the carpet and pretend everything is all right (when it's not);

- Or we can make the decision to embrace the necessary changes to be what God wants us to be and to achieve the best God wants to give us.

Thank God, I have a team who wants to achieve the highest level of victory possible for this ministry. This strong corporate desire compels us to do our best as we come to grips with the facts and make our honest report.

Once we repent for any deviation from the original vision, we return to what God first told us to do. However, if we sense the Lord leading us to make a revision or to sharpen our understanding in a way that changes our outlook, then it's time for us to *revise accordingly.*

4) REVISE

On more than one occasion, I thought I understood what the Lord wanted our ministry to do, only to find out later that I was wrong or simply misunderstood what He had put in my heart. Whenever this has happened, I've found that it's better to admit I was wrong and get back in the flow with what God's Spirit wants to do than to proceed endlessly with something I know isn't exactly correct.

> Once we repent for any deviation from the original vision, we return to what God first told us to do.

Everyone makes mistakes.

It's simply foolish to stick with the old wrong plan just because you're too embarrassed to say you made a mistake. In fact, it's pure stupidity!

The apostle Paul wrote, "For we know in part, and we prophesy in part.... For now we see through a glass, darkly; but then face to face: now I know in part; but then shall I know even as also I am known" (1 Corinthians 13:9,12).

Our understanding is not as clear today as it will be when we see Jesus face-to-face. Until that time, we will occasionally make mistakes and do things that aren't entirely correct simply because we're not able to see the full picture at the moment.

So don't waste time wallowing in eternal regret or remorse about your mistakes. If God has helped you better understand the assignment you received from heaven, it's time to revise the way you're carrying it out.

Once that revision is written down and understood by everyone involved, you need to *restructure* your church, ministry, or organization to produce the growth God wants to give you.

5) RESTRUCTURE

This is where the rubber meets the road. *Saying* you want to change and actually *doing* it are two different things. In many cases, the spirit is willing but the flesh is weak!

Revision of a vision often requires changes in the way a church, ministry, or organization operates. For example, it may require a change:

- In financial priorities.
- In personnel assignments.
- In scheduling of time.
- In office space.
- In the rank and order of the organization.

That's why there must be a reason for restructuring. It must lead somewhere. It must have a direction people can follow and a goal they can work toward. If there's no concrete reason why the change is occurring, it just becomes a nuisance that upsets a calm environment.

> Leaders must have the ability to cope with change.

Because my approach to change is so positive, I've had to work very hard to understand people's reactions to change that are different than mine. Nevertheless, leaders must have the ability to cope with change. A church, ministry, or organization is a growing entity. Anyone who is habitually resistant to change should not be considered for a top leadership position on the leadership team.

WHEN GOD FIRST SPOKE TO OUR HEARTS

Let me back up and tell you a little bit of my own story to demonstrate the changes any organization must make if it is to keep growing and expanding.

Many years ago when God first spoke to my heart and told me to begin traveling and teaching God's Word, the Holy Spirit drew both Denise's and my attention to Romans 10:18. It says, "...Yes verily, their sound went into all the earth, and their words unto the ends of the world."

When we received that *rhema* from the Spirit of God, we knew our ministry would eventually reach the ends of the world. But that dream seemed so far removed from where we were in life at that time.

We had been pastoring a small church in the state of Arkansas for several years, but now we felt led to relocate to Tulsa and look for an apartment for our small family. Once we rented and moved into our apartment, we put a big map of the

United States on the wall of our living room and began to pray every day for doors to open so our worldwide ministry could get started.

To begin with, we put a desk in the corner of the living room in our tiny apartment. Our ministry had two employees — *Denise and me!* I was the preacher, event planner, and correspondence secretary. I also single-handedly ran our tape duplication department on a duplicator that copied *three tapes* every three minutes!

Denise was busy at home but also traveled with me to sing in our meetings. She and I would load teaching tapes and luggage into our compact car and drive for hours to reach our meetings. Each night after the meeting was over, we'd join hands to pray that the offering would be big enough to buy enough gasoline to get us to the next meeting or back home. *Those were such fun and exciting times!*

Soon the ministry began to grow. We began to receive invitations to come minister the Word of God in churches throughout the central plains of the United States. It was a small beginning, but the ministry God had put in our hearts was finally beginning to spring up before our eyes.

Later, we moved out of our apartment and into a house that had two empty upstairs bedrooms. These two rooms served as our new office. We turned one bedroom into a secretarial office and the other into the workroom where we duplicated tapes. Taking into account the long hallway that linked the two rooms, this small space seemed *gigantic* to us compared to what we'd been accustomed to!

Once we'd set up our new ministry office, we hired our first full-time employee — a secretary. To get to the office, she had to come the front door of our house, walk down the hallway past our boys' bedrooms and our bedroom, and then climb the stairs to the second floor where the office was located. Our first secretary not only answered the phone, duplicated the teaching tapes, and responded to the mail — she worked as our *babysitter* as well!

As God continued to bless our work, it became evident that we could no longer work out of our home. So once more, we had to grow and change in our thinking. Renting an office was going to cost more money. But the ministry was growing too big and too fast for us to keep operating out of a home office. We held off as long as possible because our funds were tight, but at last we moved into a real office complex.

Our new office had three rooms — with enough space for three full-time employees! We had real desks, a small computer system, several telephones, and a sign out front to let everyone know that this was the new home for *Rick Renner Ministries.*

PUBLISHING MY BOOKS REQUIRED
MANY CHANGES IN OUR MINISTRY

The next big change in my ministry occurred after holding a series of meetings in Tulsa, Oklahoma, for my dear friend, Pastor Bob Yandian of Grace Fellowship Church. Bob urged me to put the messages I had preached into book form. He told me,

"You've got to get this message into print, Rick. It will make a great book. People need this message."

At Bob's encouragement, I went to my computer and started to put my message into print. My first book, *Seducing Spirits and Doctrines of Demons,* was a best-seller. It sold out of its first printing in thirty days. Then it sold out of the second printing, third printing, fourth printing, and so on. Next, I wrote my second book, *Living in the Combat Zone.* It, too, became a best-seller.

We could hardly keep these books in print because the orders were coming so fast. It was every author's dream! My heart was thrilled when I came to the office and saw the stacks and stacks of orders for my books. When I wrote my third book, the same thing happened again. Growth was coming faster and faster. *We were racing to keep up with it.*

Each day our post office box was filled with letters from people who wanted to obtain more information about our ministry, order our various tape series, or invite us to come preach in church meetings, seminars, and conventions. The barriers that once had held us back were being broken, and the blessings of heaven were being abundantly poured upon us.

To accommodate this growth, I knew we had to make some significant changes in the way we were doing things in our office. The method of operation we were used to could *not* sustain the growth the Lord was about to send us. So we relocated our office to a larger space. We hired additional staff members. This meant more finances and a bigger budget. *It also meant that I would have to change.*

LEARNING TO DELEGATE
WAS A BIG CHANGE TO MY STYLE

My level of involvement at the office had been *intense.* I wanted to be informed of every little detail, such as how much ministry stationery to order, how many blank audio cassettes to order, and so on.

I was so involved in every little detail that I personally designed the covers for my tape series; I called and confirmed meetings with pastors; and I ordered all the tickets for our plane travel.

When we were first getting started, I *had* to take care of all these practical responsibilities because we didn't have staff members to do it. But as the ministry grew and finances increased so we could hire staff, I didn't need to keep doing these things. I was free to devote my attention to other responsibilities, such as praying, studying, writing, and producing new teaching materials.

However, there was one problem! I had been responsible for these more practical tasks for so long that, when it was no longer necessary for me to do them, *I could hardly let them all go!* Even though staff members were hired to fulfill these responsibilities, I hovered over them to make sure they did it as I would do it. I hovered so closely, I made it hard for them to do their work. My excessive hovering also crippled my ability to fulfill my own responsibilities of praying, studying, and preparing to teach. *Letting go was so hard for me!*

You see, my staff members were more than employees; they were also my friends. I enjoyed floating in and out of their offices to talk to them about their spouses, their children, their dreams, and their work. So like a magnet, I was pulled right into the middle of everything — *even into the middle of matters I didn't need to be directly involved in anymore.* It was time for someone else to take responsibility for those matters, and it was time for me to move up to a new spiritual level. *The problem wasn't the staff. The problem was that I didn't want to let go!*

By this time, I was traveling all over the United States, preaching four hundred times a year. I was also continually in the process of writing another book. In addition, I was a husband and a daddy to three wonderful boys. It was a physical impossibility for me to do all this and keep track of the practical details of the ministry simultaneously. Something had to change.

I finally realized I couldn't maintain my intense level of involvement in the office and travel full time too. It was a physical impossibility. This meant I had to learn to *delegate.*

Learning to delegate is essential if a leader wants his church, ministry, business, or organization to keep growing. Many churches, ministries, businesses, and organizations never reach their maximum poten-

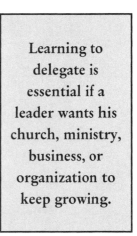

Learning to delegate is essential if a leader wants his church, ministry, business, or organization to keep growing.

tial because they don't delegate key responsibilities to others or trust others to take leadership roles. That's why it's so essential for the leadership of a growing organization to keep an open mind about learning new and better ways of doing things.

Learning to trust the team the Lord gave me was a key to the growth of our organization.

Leaders who are fearful to let go and allow others in their organization to take a leading role often prevent the potential impact of the organization from ever being realized. These leaders may have ideas, concepts, and solutions that could radically change the lives of multitudes. But because they insist on staying involved in every little detail, they limit themselves and hinder the growth of their organization. *Their control is too strict to allow for growth.*

I, too, could have tried to keep my finger on every little detail of my ministry. But if I had, it would have been *impossible* for the ministry to have kept growing as it has over the years.

KEEP ON CHANGING, KEEP ON GROWING

There are many factors that encourage growth. For instance, another essential ingredient for growth is a leader's willingness to accept new financial responsibilities.

The need for additional finances is so big and scary to some leaders that they often rationalize their own inaction, saying that the benefits of growth are too risky. Rather than press forward to achieve more, they retreat into a mode of self-preservation. For them, *maintaining* is more important than *gaining.*

Denise and I had made many big changes in our thinking and believing since we had left Arkansas. But just because we had gained a little ground didn't mean the journey was completed. If we were to keep growing, we would have to keep changing.

Years later, God gave us a vision to reach the entire former USSR and Europe with television. This new vision necessitated more growth and additional changes in our way of thinking, believing, and acting.

Then came the day I recognized the apostolic call on my life. This revelation required me to change again in the way I viewed myself and our ministry. I had to come up higher, make adjustments in my thinking, and start releasing others to step into positions of ministry that I had previously thought would always be mine.

If I was going to fulfill what God had called me to do, I had no choice but to change in both my thinking and acting. And I know this isn't the end of change for me. As long as I serve the Lord, He will be calling me from one level of glory to the next (2 Corinthians 3:18).

Yes, change is difficult for all of us. But solid, stable, dependable growth will not occur in our lives or ministries without change. As creatures of habit, our flesh likes to hold on to the way things are. We don't want to be disturbed by anything new and different. But if we intend to keep making significant progress and advances in life, we must reckon with the fact that we will be growing and making changes as long as we live on this earth.

Babies change as they get older. Children change when they become teenagers. Teenagers change when they become young men and women. People change again and again and again during the course of their lifetime.

Change is normal for anything that grows. Yet our flesh cringes at the thought of letting go of what is comfortable and known in order to reach to a new level of attainment.

At times you may be tempted to view "change" merely as "risk" when you begin climbing to new heights in your church, ministry, organization, or business. Some of those risks may be *real.* Some may be *imagined.*

Regardless, don't let yourself resist the changes and adjustments that God puts on your heart to make. And don't give someone a high-priority place of leadership on your team who stubbornly drags his feet and always resists change. This type of leader would only pull you down and keep your ministry or organization from making significant advances.

> Don't give someone a high-priority place of leadership on your team who stubbornly drags his feet and always resists change.

As you choose leadership for your team, be sure to select people who are open to change and who can embrace steps toward progress. It is essential for you to surround yourself with this type of people if you intend to lead your ministry or organization to the highest heights possible to attain.

QUESTIONS FOR PERSONAL GROWTH OR GROUP DISCUSSION

1. What steps can you take to help your team members follow you unreservedly through all the "growing pains" of your church, ministry, or organization?

2. What should you do when a faithful team member is having difficulty accepting the changes you are trying to implement?

3. What are the five steps you need to take if your church, ministry, or organization hasn't been growing the way it should?

4. Take some time to reexamine the original vision God placed in your heart, Have you strayed from that original vision in any way? Are there areas in which God may be leading you to revise the way you are fulfilling that vision?

5. Why is learning how to delegate so essential to the growth of your organization?

NOTES:

_____

_____

_____

_____

_____

_____

_____

_____

_____

_____

_____

_____

_____

_____

_____

_____

_____

_____

_____

_____

_____

_____

HOW DOES THE PROSPECTIVE LEADER GET ALONG WITH OTHER PEOPLE?

e once had an employee who held a very strategic position in our ministry. However, this man was a constant source of heartache because he was so difficult to get along with from day to day.

When the man first came to work for us, there didn't seem to be any problem. On the surface, everything looked fine. But as time passed, it became apparent that this particular staff member had a deeper problem of which no one knew. He could not get along with people.

In fact, he was so nit-picky about other people that no one was ever able to be good enough to meet his unrealistic standards. As one employee told me, *"He's so difficult! If we don't agree with him and see everything exactly his way, he becomes so rude!"*

Indeed, this staff member was rude. He was also ill-mannered, short-tempered, coarse, curt, harsh, argumentative, and combative in his dealings with other people on staff. All someone had to do was accidentally look at him the wrong way, and he would fly off the handle and maliciously lambast them.

AN ANGRY MAN STIRS UP STRIFE

Proverbs 29:22 says, "An angry man stirreth up strife, and a furious man aboundeth in transgression."

I'll never forget the day I walked into the ministry office and found this employee screaming at the receptionist because he didn't like the way she greeted him when he came into the office that morning. When I told him to get control of himself, he stormed off in a state of fury. The entire staff was on pins and needles. *It was an intolerable situation.*

This situation was also a paradox to me. One moment this man could be so charming that the whole staff would try to overlook his negative behavior and believe the best about him. But then the very next moment he could turn as quarrelsome as an angry hornet. This was a true-life scenario of *Dr. Jekyll and Mr.Hyde*!

Had I known that the man had this problem when I asked him to join our team, I never would have done so. But I felt pressure to find someone to fill his position, so I quickly hired him without knowing a lot about him. It was a mistake I seriously regretted later. I was perturbed at myself for violating my own principles and hiring this man too quickly, simply because I was impressed by his talents and abilities.

Cast Out the Scorner, and
Contention Shall Cease

The situation with this staff member grew worse day by day.

Proverbs 22:10 says, "Cast out the scorner, and contention shall go out; yea, strife and reproach shall cease." If this man couldn't learn to take control of his temper and work peacefully alongside other people on our team, I had no choice but to remove him.

However, this man was an important person to our ministry because his job was of such a specialized nature. He wouldn't be easy to replace. At that particular time, our organization was very dependent on his skills and abilities. Had we lost him at that exact moment, it would have crippled the entire outreach of *Rick Renner Ministries.*

This employee knew this was the case and believed he was irreplaceable to our organization. He used this as leverage to do whatever he wanted to do and to act however he chose to act, regardless how his behavior affected other people.

I tried to spend time with the man to bring him closer to my heart and make him more central to the team. When I prayed with him, I could see that he really loved me and our ministry. But whenever he dealt with people, it was like a run-in with the devil himself.

He was so volatile that even I wondered, *What kind of mood will he be in when he shows up today? Will he be a delight to work with, or will he put us through another grueling day of torture?*

This man had come from a difficult background. He was raised in a home with no father, where he had struggled economically and emotionally through most of his childhood and adolescence. Then he was sent to a military school as a young man, where strict rules were harshly applied.

As this man told me his story, I could see that he hadn't been shown any tenderness in the developmental stages of his life Because of this, I made exceptions for his behavior.

Time and again, I met with this employee to discuss his attitude toward other people. I wanted to help him and salvage him from the destructive attitudes working in his life. I knew if he didn't conquer these feelings of hostility, it would harass him for the rest of his life and negatively affect his future.

Talent nearly oozed from the pores of this man's skin. He could speak, sing, and dance, and in rare moments, he could preach like an evangelist on fire. Oh, how I wanted to help him so he'd be a blessing and not be rejected because of his belligerent spirit toward other people!

When I met with him to discuss these personality difficulties, I didn't cherish conflict or long for him to unleash his anger toward me. The only reason I made myself sit down to talk with him is that I loved him and wanted to see this situation redeemed.

But rather than receive my words of correction with an open heart, the man was unyielding in his attitude. *Obstinate, headstrong, bullheaded, stubborn,* and *disregarding* are just a few of the words I'd use to describe how others perceived him and how he acted toward me.

WHAT SHOULD I DO?

I knew if I fired the man, our work would be drastically affected. We didn't have anyone else with his skills — skills that were essential if we were to accomplish the tasks set before us.

If I held him accountable for his wrong behavior, I knew everyone in the office — including me — would bear the brunt of his bad attitude for days. His silence after confrontation was a form of manipulation he used to make sure his feelings were known.

So I rolled the matter over and over in my mind. I wanted to walk in kindness and patience, but I didn't want him to paralyze our organization either. I began asking myself:

- What should I do?
- Should I deal with the problem?
- Should I fire him and look for his replacement?
- Or should I overlook it and hope for the best?

What made it even harder was the fact that I knew this man loved me. He told me, "Rick, you're like a father to me." But he didn't treat me like a father, nor did he respond to our ministry like it was his family. Rather, he acted as if he were on one side and we were on the other.

There was no sense of "teamwork" or "family feelings" between this man and anyone else in the ministry. He was like a foreigner in our midst. He kept a distance between himself and the rest of the team members, refusing to allow anyone to get close.

This situation produced a great conflict within me because I had no doubt that the man wanted to do an excellent job. His work itself was superior, and his results were outstanding. However, he was an island to himself because *no one* in the ministry wanted any kind of further contact with him.

In time, I had to let the man go because he was totally unable to work with other people.

WHY DID I ENDURE THIS SITUATION FOR SO LONG?

I endured this situation for several years because I believed in this man's potential. I also wanted to see him set free from the hurts that bound him up and made him act so caustic.

I knew the man was chained in his own invisible prison. When he put others down, magnifying their faults and weaknesses, he did it to somehow picture himself a little higher than they were. It was a sick way to feel better about himself.

Even he acknowledged that he had spent his whole lifetime trying to prove he was worth something. But in his efforts to prove his own worth, he had placed unrealistic goals on himself that condemned him to repeated failure in his own eyes.

The perfection the man expected of himself was unrealistic. It was impossible for any human being to attain the perfection he sought. And if others weren't as perfect as he thought they should be, then he took it upon himself to become their judge too. This is one reason his treatment of others was so cruel and vindictive.

This man could have been helped if he'd had a heart that was willing to receive correction and work on the areas of his life that needed to be changed. But because he refused to deal with the defects that alienated him from the rest of the team, he was eventually dismissed. And although we didn't know at first how we'd survive without his skills, God brought us a precious replacement — a person who, although less talented, had a heart to learn, grow, and work as a part of the team.

Finally, that one department of our ministry that had been so distant from everyone else became a vital part of the entire organization. Our entire staff was once more at peace, and the joy of serving the Lord together as a team was restored.

One Disjointed Person Can Throw The Whole Team Into a State of Confusion

When you select a person for a leadership position, be sure you're inviting someone into your inner circle who has the ability to work alongside the other team members. One disjointed person can throw your entire organization off balance. The situation can become so painful that you'll regret you ever invited that person to join your team.

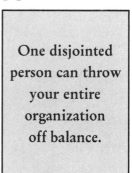

One disjointed person can throw your entire organization off balance.

Timothy had a problem with leaders in his church who were difficult to handle and who struggled with submitting to authority. Paul referred to this difficulty when he wrote to Timothy and said, "From which some having swerved have turned aside unto vain jangling" (1 Timothy 1:6).

The words "turned aside" come from the Greek word *ektrepomai*. This word *ektrepomai is* a medical term that describes *a bone that's out of joint.*

When a bone is out of joint, it's a very difficult and painful experience. Although that bone is still located inside the body, it isn't properly connected. And because that one out-of-joint bone isn't connected correctly, it becomes a major source of pain and irritation, sending signals of pain throughout the entire body. Nearly every movement of the body is affected as that out-of-joint bone screams misery throughout a person's central nervous system.

This is the image Paul had in mind when he used the word *ektrepomai* to describe unruly, difficult people. Although these people are saved and valuable to God, they are a constant source of pain and irritation to the entire organization because they are "out of joint" with the rest of the body of believers.

A sincere act of repentance would snap these out-of-joint people back into their rightful place so they could begin to function properly and become a working member of the team. But no one can make them repent and get their attitude right. It's a decision only *they* have the power to make for themselves. And once they make this decision, they can once again become a benefit and a joy to the entire organization.

If you have a person working under your authority who is loaded with gifts and talents but is constantly "out of joint" with everyone else, you have a serious problem on your hands. Talk to that person. Explain to him why his attitude is wrong. Do everything you can to snap him back into the godly attitude and behavior he ought to be displaying as a member of your team.

But if he refuses to listen and continues to upset your peaceful environment, rejecting your counsel to deal with his wrong attitudes toward other people, I suggest that you start looking for a replacement. And if you haven't given that person a position yet, don't do it. Wait for God to send you someone who knows how to get along with other people.

ASK THESE QUESTIONS
BEFORE MAKING A FINAL DECISION

So when choosing people to be a part of your team, don't forget to deal with this serious question: *How do these candidates get along with other people?*

I recommend that you ask the following questions before you seal the deal and make a final decision about bringing new people on to your team:

- How do these potential leaders get along with other people?

- What happened at their previous job?

- What reason do they give for leaving their previous place of employment?

- Is there a reason they left their last church and have now come to your church?

- Are you sure they didn't have a rebellion problem with their previous pastor or his leadership team?

- What kind of testimony do these potential leaders have with their families?

- What kind of testimony do these candidates have with their fellow employees?

- Do the candidates' fellow employees enjoy working with them and perceive them as real team players?

- Are the potential leaders known to be kind and peaceable to other people, or are they temperamental and hard to get along with?

- Do the candidates carry grudges against people from their past and refuse to forgive them?

- Have the potential leaders demonstrated a willingness to be wrong and to admit that others may have a better way of doing things than they do?

- Do they understand authority and submission? Do they know how to properly respond to their leaders?

- Do the candidates gossip about other people?

- Do they talk behind people's backs or talk about other people's business when they ought to be minding their own business?

- How do the potential leaders talk to other people? Do they demonstrate respect?

- Do the candidates show that they appreciate what others do on the job, or do they talk only of themselves and their own accomplishments?

- Are the candidates able to say, "I'm sorry" when they do something that isn't right?

The answers to these questions may reveal whether or not you want to place these potential leaders into leadership positions on your team. The answers will also give you good insight into what kind of people these candidates really are — whether they are team players or islands unto themselves.

Once you find the answers to these questions, don't shut your eyes to the truth. Even if you don't like what you see or hear, the answers may save you from making a dreadful mistake regarding your leadership team.

> Never overlook this question: "How well does this person get along with other people?"

Take it from one who has learned the hard way — never overlook this question: "How well does this person get along with other people?" The answer to this question will help you make much wiser choices as you select additional people to join your leadership team.

QUESTIONS FOR PERSONAL GROWTH
OR GROUP DISCUSSION

1. Can you think of an "out-of-joint" person with whom you have worked in the past? How did that person's attitude and behavior affect his coworkers and supervisors? How did he or she affect the atmosphere in the workplace?

2. Consider the options you would face if you had a person working under you whose talents seemed indispensable but who had problems getting along with his coworkers. What would be your wisest course of action?

3. Suppose you have to correct a person whose bad attitude has caused disruption in your ministry or organization. If that person refuses to listen and continues his "out-of-joint" behavior, what should be the next step you take to correct the situation?

4. What outward signs should you look for in a potential leader's life to help you determine whether or not he or she can get along with other people?

5. As you use these same criteria to examine yourself, how would you describe your own ability to get along well with others?

NOTES:

_____

_____

_____

_____

_____

_____

_____

_____

_____

_____

_____

_____

_____

_____

_____

_____

_____

_____

_____

_____

_____

HOW DOES THIS PERSON YOU'RE CONSIDERING RESPOND TO CORRECTION?

*P*erhaps nothing gives you quicker insight into a person's character than how he responds to correction.

If a person interrupts you, argues, and wants to defend himself, it's usually a sign that he has a difficult time submitting to authority. I've found that 99.9% of the time, this type of person will be difficult to deal with on every level.

If a person has an open heart and is teachable, you will quickly see it. *A right or wrong attitude is easily discerned.* When you sit down to correct a potential leader, it won't take too long to figure out which attitude this person possesses. If he has a right attitude, it will be visible as he receives your correction and thanks you for taking the time to show him what's wrong and how to improve himself.

I recently spoke a word of correction to one of my leaders that in my opinion would have been very hard to receive. His response to me was so right and so receptive that it revealed his heart to me. It was more important to him to be in a right relationship with me than it was to prove he was right and I was wrong. He received what I had to say.

When a potential leader responds in such a positive, receptive way, it is a strong indicator of the kind of team member this person will be. It reveals his level of understanding of authority and submission and how respectful he is toward his superiors.

> I've found that one of the most revealing ways to discover what's in a person's heart is to see how he responds to correction.

I've found that one of the most revealing ways to discover what's in a person's heart is to see how he responds to correction. Not only do I watch to see how he responds at that exact moment, but I also keep an eye on him to see if he took my correction to heart and changed what he was doing wrong. *I want to know how deeply he took my words into his soul.* Let me give you an example of what I mean.

A DIFFICULT EXPERIENCE
WITH A STAFF MEMBER

In the early days of our ministry in the former Soviet Union, we had an American staff member who moaned and groaned all the time because he was working so hard and was making such great sacrifices for the Lord. It was true that he was working hard, but so were all the rest of us. Launching a ministry in the former Soviet Union was no small task.

I agreed with this staff member when he told me that he and his wife were facing hardships they had never faced before. *However, I also knew they weren't alone in this predicament.* Who wasn't facing difficult hardships in the former USSR at that time?

Gorbachev's plan of *perestroika* had just miserably failed. (*Perestroika* is a common Russian word used by the government to refer to the "restructuring" or "rebuilding" of the communist system.) When *perestroika* failed, it was devastating for everyone.

The grocery stores were left practically empty. The pharmacies were bare of the most essential medical products. And because the service stations had no gas to sell, entire cities were left without the ability to even use an automobile.

The most basic products — sugar, flour, milk, and eggs — were difficult to find. Even when they were found in a local grocery store, they could be bought only with state-issued ration coupons. Obtaining those ration coupons was therefore the first step in buying needed food items. However, that proved to be a huge challenge because everyone wanted them.

This staff member's never-ending gripes about how much he and his wife were suffering absolutely *puzzled* me. All he could do was think about himself. He couldn't even see that everyone was dealing with hardships, not just he and his wife.

The truth is, this man's family was living at a much higher level of comfort and privilege than his neighbors or fellow workers at the office. In fact, because he complained so much, everyone rallied to help his family get over the hump they were experiencing. But no matter how much people did for this staff member and his wife, they continued to moan and groan about how bad life was and how much they had sacrificed for the Lord.

One day our ministry administrator came into my office, sat down, and just looked at me as if he was totally frustrated. When I asked him what was wrong, he said, "I've just about had it with that man's mouth and constant complaining about everything. I don't want to hear one more thing about how much he has sacrificed for the Lord!"

The administrator continued, "If he comes in here complaining one more time, I don't know what I'm going to do. I'm so tired of listening to a grown man act like such a baby. He knew the conditions over here when he agreed to come!"

As I listened to the administrator, I remembered the day this staff member first came to see me in the United States. I vividly recalled what he told me that day.

He said, *"I believe God is calling me to move to the former USSR with you to help get your ministry up and going. I'm willing to make any sacrifice, even to work without pay if needed, just for the privilege of being a part of such a history-making event."*

At that time, my family had already lived in the former Soviet Union for quite a while. We knew the inconveniences and hardships this man and his wife would face if they joined us on the other side of the world. They'd have to deal with challenges such as:

- Standing in long lines for bread and other basic food items.

- Enduring weeks of having the water turned off to their neighborhood.

- Facing the difficulties of finding transportation, dealing with the Russian language, and overcoming cultural barriers.

- Learning how to live on the Russian ruble, which was constantly fluctuating in value from day to day.

- Navigating through the incredible political instability that existed at that time.

All this was a part of what this family would experience if they moved to the former Soviet Union. Knowing full well what lay ahead of them, I asked them over and over again if they were certain God had called them to join our team. I wanted to give them every opportunity to back out, so I asked them:

- Do you understand the amount of work this commitment will require of you?

- Are you both in full agreement with this decision?

- Do you understand the economic situation you will be moving into, and do you agree to live in it with a grateful heart?

- Are you able to be away from your family for a long period of time without getting too homesick?

- Are you truly committed to work through all the cultural differences and learn how to operate with an unstable currency?

- This is the amount of money we can pay you. Are you satisfied with this salary, or will this be a problem for you later on down the road?

This man assured me: "Yes, we are willing to work hard. It's clear to us that it will take a lot of effort. We understand it may be the hardest thing we've ever done in our lives.

"The salary you've offered to pay us is wonderful. The truth is, we're so excited about being a part of this opportunity that we feel like we ought to be paying *you*. And we fully understand that we will be moving into a situation that is economically and politically unstable. Yes, Rick, we get the picture, and we are still confident that God is calling us to do this."

TIME IS A GREAT REVEALER
OF WHO PEOPLE REALLY ARE

Months had passed since that first conversation, and the hard reality of this couple's decision was beginning to dawn on them. Yes, life was difficult for them, but theirs was no special case. Life was difficult for the entire population in the former USSR.

The biggest issue that this couple kept bringing up again and again was how hard it had been for them to leave their families in order to help in our ministry. However, I hadn't asked them to leave their families — they had come to me and said they "felt the call of God" to move to that region of the world and join our team.

At first, I tried to help this couple, remembering how difficult it had been when our family first moved to that part of the world. It had been quite a shock to our American way of thinking and lifestyle when we first moved there, so Denise and

I felt great mercy and sympathy for all the struggles this man and his wife were going through.

We also understood how difficult it was to live so far away from family. At that time, an international phone call had to be ordered three days in advance. That meant we couldn't even pick up the phone to call home when we wanted to. And when our phone connection to the United States was finally made, the connection was often so poor that we couldn't hear the person on the other end of the line. This meant we had to order *another* call and wait *another* three days before we could try to call home again!

In light of these conditions in the former Soviet Union, feelings of homesickness seemed normal for anyone who had just moved to that side of the world. So we tried to comfort this couple as they worked through their transition. But after a while, I realized that no matter how much we comforted them, they would not be comforted!

I wondered if this staff member and his wife had forgotten the fact that every member of our team, whether American, Latvian, Russian, or Ukrainian, was living far from his or her family and not native to the city where we were working and serving at that time.

The USSR encompassed eleven time zones, so just because a staff member spoke Russian didn't mean he felt at home in the city where our ministry was located. He could have been ten time zones away from his family — much farther away from home than the moaning, groaning staff member who had "felt the call of God" to come from America in order to help us get our ministry started.

All of us were making sacrifices in order to do what we were doing. All of us were facing equal hardships. But the only ones who complained about it were this man and his wife. Everyone else "bit the bullet," accepted the challenge, and made the best of the situation.

This man would bewail, *"I've left my family and moved so far from home. Do you understand what a great sacrifice I've made for the Lord and for this ministry? Do you realize what great sacrifices I've made by moving here to work in this ministry?"*

The time finally came when the entire staff began to run out of patience. Everyone got fed up with hearing this couple sing the same sad song every day at the office. I could see that feelings of resentment toward these two were growing among staff members as appreciation for their work decreased. In the end, I knew I would have to sit down with this man and wife *again* to discuss their sour attitudes because they were adversely affecting so many people in our organization.

SACRIFICES WITH STRIFE

It was true that this staff member and his wife had made sacrifices. The problem was that they hadn't made them with joy. They kept records of their sacrifices; they told everyone about their sacrifices; and they got upset if we didn't magnify how much they had suffered and given up to come work on our team.

Proverbs 17:1 says, "Better is a dry morsel, and quietness therewith, than an house full of sacrifices with strife."

I can't see how the Lord got any pleasure out of the "sacrifices" this man and wife had made because they resented every bit of it. They were living their entire lives with a frown on their faces. Every little thing that happened seemed to annoy and upset them. Even worse, they held over our heads the fact that they had made this "great sacrifice" — as if we had made them do it!

I knew I needed to sit down and correct this staff member. His behavior had gone over the limit. However, I dreaded the prospect of correcting the man because he had such a strong personality and had been so incredibly negative to everyone in the office — *including me.*

I deliberated for days before I sat down with him. Finally, I pulled up my chair to his desk and said, "I need to talk to you about your attitude." But before I could even get started, he was already putting up a wall of defense that made it impossible for me to deal with him.

Talking to that man was like talking to a brick wall. He became argumentative and defensive. I kept thinking, *Wait a minute! I didn't come here to fight with him today! I came here to be a help and a blessing!*

At first, I thought he was being defensive because he was embarrassed. Then I thought that perhaps he felt humiliated because he already knew his behavior had been wrong.

But after a few minutes, I could see that he simply didn't have an open heart. He didn't like where he was or what he was doing. He didn't even like me. My attempt to speak a word of correction into his life was a total waste of his and my time.

How this man responded to me revealed the kind of heart he had. I knew he would never last long in our ministry. I wouldn't have to eliminate him — he would remove himself.

Had the man opened his heart and allowed me to speak into his life, I could have helped him. But he wasn't open to receiving input from anyone and was therefore destined to go through a series of mishaps and serious mistakes of his own making. However, all those mistakes could have been avoided if only he had allowed someone to be a friend and speak the truth to him.

Eventually this man left our ministry. When he decided to leave, I didn't beg him to stay longer. I was relieved he was leaving our midst because it was such a constant hassle to work with him.

BRINGING CORRECTION IS HARD TO DO

As a pastor, I can tell you that when I sit down to speak correction into someone's life, it isn't something I relish to do because it can be so awkward. Therefore, I earnestly pray and seek God's face before I proceed.

I don't know of a single pastor, parent, or employer who delights in bringing someone correction. *Giving correction is hard to do — and so is receiving correction!*

It must have been difficult for Timothy to give correction as well because Paul had to write to him and give him instructions about how to do it. When Paul wrote to Timothy, the younger man was facing serious leadership problems in his own church at Ephesus. Some members of his leadership team were teaching false doctrine. It appears that they were also demonstrating a rebellious attitude toward Timothy as their pastor.

It seems that Timothy wrote to Paul and asked for suggestions on how to deal with the problem. Paul wrote back and gave Timothy sound advice that is still applicable to us today.

Let's take a few moments to look at several key words Paul used when he wrote Timothy and explained how to give correction to someone who is under one's sphere of authority. The words Paul used make it obvious that Timothy wasn't thrilled about this particular pastoral duty.

PAUL'S ADVICE TO SPIRITUAL LEADERS
ABOUT HOW TO BRING CORRECTION

Second Timothy 2:24 says, "And the servant of the Lord must not strive; but be gentle unto all men, apt to teach, patient." Notice that Paul called Timothy "the servant of the Lord." The word "servant" is the Greek word *doulos*. It describes *a bondslave who is bound to do what he is told to do, regardless of what he thinks about it.* His position is not to argue with his superior but to faithfully execute what he is told to do.

This means that Timothy was not his own boss. As the bondslave of the Lord, his position was to hear what the Lord told him to do and then to execute it no matter what he felt or thought about it. He was to faithfully carry out the Lord's orders.

It is significant that Paul used this word when he instructed Timothy to deal with problem-makers in his church. It tells us that Timothy didn't want to do it. Paul was reminding him that as the servant of the Lord, Timothy didn't have a choice regarding how he was going to handle the situation.

Timothy was the chief leader of the church. Therefore, it was his responsibility to step into his leadership position and act with the authority and responsibility God had given him. No one else had the position or power to set things in order. Whether he wanted to do it or not, it was time for Timothy to step up to the plate and start to play according to God's rules.

DON'T LET YOURSELF GET DRAGGED INTO A WAR OF WORDS

God had placed Timothy in this leading role, so Paul endeavored to help the younger minister out by giving him some solid suggestions regarding how to give correction. These suggestions are applicable to any leader who finds himself in Timothy's position.

First, Paul told Timothy that "...the servant of the Lord must not strive...:" The word "strive" is the Greek word *mache*. Pay close attention to the meaning of this word.

The word *mache* was generally used to describe *armed combatants,* such as those who fought to the death with sharpened swords. The word *mache* also depicted *close, personal, hand-to-hand combat* — the kind that usually ended with two people in a deadly, mangled mess on the floor.

By the time the New Testament was written, the word *mache* was used to portray *people who have an argumentative spirit and like to engage in a war of words.* This type of person doesn't swing a sword. He wages war, squabbles, and fights with other people using *words.*

When you sit down to bring correction into a person's life, you are doing it because you want to help. That's why it can be so frustrating when that person tries to turn the tables on you and pick a fight instead of receiving the correction you are trying to give him. In fact, if you aren't in control of your emotions at that moment, you may have to fight the temptation to "jump in the ring" and "slug it out"!

This can be one of the most frustrating experiences you go through as a leader. You seek God for His wisdom on how to deal with a problem person. But when you sit down to help that person, his reaction to you is so disrespectful that you feel like you've just been spit on!

Wait a minute! You sat down with that person to discuss his problem — and now you're defending yourself for trying to help him! He's attacking you, trying to turn this into an opportunity to correct you instead.

There is no winner in this kind of conversation. If the other person's heart is so closed to you that he would argue and show you that much disrespect, it's better to leave the table until another time — that is, if you ever choose to come back to the table!

Suppose I take the time to sit down with a prospective candidate to show him where he's wrong and how things can be better. He responds by speaking sharply to me, attacking me, putting up a wall of defense, or turning the conversation around to point out my weaknesses instead of his. When that happens, *I already know that person will not be a part of my leadership team at this particular time.*

Maybe he'll be a part of the team later, but his actions and words have revealed something to me that prevents me from wanting him as a part of my team right now. Someone who calls me his spiritual authority but doesn't allow me to speak into his life without an argument is not a person I want to work closely with.

> Someone who calls me his spiritual authority but doesn't allow me to speak into his life without an argument is not a person I want to work closely with.

If you feel led to continue your talk with a combative person, first let that person finish "having his say." Then proceed according to the Lord's leading.

Paul was giving good, solid advice to all leaders — advice that's still applicable today to you and me. *He was warning us NOT to get dragged into a war of words when we sit down to bring correction into someone's life.*

STAY IN CONTROL OF YOURSELF

Paul went on to say that the servant of the Lord must be "gentle."

The word "gentle" is the Greek word *epios*. It denotes a *behavior that is mild, gentle, or kind.* It carries the idea of being *mild-mannered* as opposed to *easily angered.*

Paul was telling us that we cannot let our feelings take control when we are verbally assaulted by someone under our authority. That person obviously doesn't understand submission and authority, or he wouldn't act like that.

> **We cannot let our feelings take control when we are verbally assaulted by someone under our authority. Getting upset doesn't make it better.**

Getting upset doesn't make it better. It is far better to determine before the conversation even begins to remain calm, gentle, kind, and mild-mannered, no matter how the other person responds.

If you start screaming and fighting back, you only demonstrate your own lack of spiritual maturity. Strength isn't revealed by how loud you talk or how gruff you appear to another person. In fact, great inner strength and fortitude is often manifested through silence.

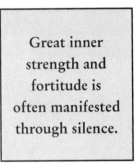

> **Great inner strength and fortitude is often manifested through silence.**

When you let your feelings get the best of you, you lower yourself to the level of that difficult person. So remember — you're in charge, not the other person. Don't let yourself grunt and growl, even if he does. If you end up in the dirt, you'll give the person even more ammunition with which to accuse you.

So keep yourself on a higher level. Stay in control of your emotions when dealing with an argumentative person.

TAKE THEM TO 'SCHOOL' AND SHOW THEM
WHERE THEY'RE WRONG

Paul also said the servant of the Lord must be "apt to teach." The Greek word is *didasktikos*. It describes *one who is skillful in teaching or instruction.*

You see, if God calls on you to speak correction into someone else's life, you must be able to *explicitly explain* to that person what he's done wrong and how he should make it right. He needs to see the situation as clearly as possible. Don't speak in vague, ambiguous terms, or he won't have a clue about what you're trying to tell him. Just present him with concrete facts and illustrations, and he'll be able to see and understand your point. Always remember — the more examples you can give as you correct him, the more you'll help him understand the point you're making.

Also, don't point out the person's incorrect behavior as if it were just a matter of your opinion versus his opinion. Take him to the Word. Teach the person principles that will make the issue absolutely clear to him. That's the best way to keep him from repeating the same mistake.

Receiving correction is hard for anyone. It's embarrassing. It's often hurtful. It's humbling. So make sure you give the person enough of the Word — with vivid scriptural examples and principles — to help him swallow what you have to say.

Consider this: How would you want someone to correct *you?*

- Harshly?
- Tenderly?

- Without explanation or teaching?
- With full instruction and a heart of mercy?
- As a friend instead of a foe?

Correction is hard both to give and to receive. That's why both giver and receiver need to do everything they can to make a time of correction as successful as possible.

In particular, the giver of correction should come to the receiver with the full picture, with clear explanation, with solid teaching from the Word, *and with a positive approach toward turning the situation around.* These elements of correction always help the medicine go down a little easier.

This is why Paul said the servant of the Lord must be "apt to teach."

HAVE A TOLERANT ATTITUDE

Paul also said that the servant of the Lord must be "patient." The Greek word for "patient" is *aneksikakos.* This word is a compound of the words *anechomai* and *kakos.* The word *anechomai* means *to endure patiently, to bear with, or to have a tolerant attitude toward someone or something.* The word *kakos* is the Greek word for *evil* or for *something that is bad.*

When these two words are compounded into the word *aneksikakos* as they are in this verse, it portrays *an attitude that is tolerant and that bears with a bad, depraved, or an evil response.* Paul was telling Timothy (and us!) to *put up* with the person's reaction whether it's good or bad.

In Galatians 6:1, Paul tells us, "Brethren, if a man be overtaken in a fault, ye which are spiritual, restore such an one in the spirit of meekness; considering thyself, lest thou also be tempted."

So as you begin the process of bringing correction into a person's life, *put yourself in his shoes.* If you were the one sitting there, would it be easy or would it be difficult for you to hear what is being said? Would you feel super about this meeting, or would you feel a little embarrassed?

> As you begin the process of bringing correction into a person's life, put yourself in his shoes. If you were the one sitting there, would it be easy or would it be difficult for you to hear what is being said?

If the person you are correcting acts closed or puts up a wall of defense at first, it may be that he's just embarrassed or reacting out of insecurity. Therefore, don't leave the table and stop the conversation unless you can see that he's definitely just being combative and completely closed to your input. In order to discern the true situation, you need to be patient and slow in judging his reaction to your correction.

Take your time. Let the person talk. If he's just reacting in embarrassment or from the shock of being corrected, bear with him until he's able to work through his emotions and really hear what you have to say.

This is *exactly* what the apostle Paul was talking about when he said that the servant of the Lord must be "patient."

The Most Important Question

The most important question is not always "Who's right or wrong?" Often, it's "What is the attitude and response of the person being corrected?" You see, even if I'm wrong in the correction I give to a person, he should still respect and consider what I have to say if he claims that God has placed him under my pastoral care.

If a potential leader doesn't know how to respond to your authority or how to receive correction from you without getting angry and upset, you can know that this person is a potential problem. I strongly advise you not to invite that potential hurricane into your team too quickly. If you do, you'll have a problem on your hands all the time!

Perhaps that person will make a great team member later on down the road. But if he doesn't have the maturity to receive correction right now, you won't have any authority in his life once you give him a position on your leadership team.

So don't make a decision you'll regret later. Let that person grow. Let him learn a little more about life. Let him serve in the local church and learn how to work alongside other people. It may be that he just needs some more time to mature before you give him such a lofty position of power and responsibility.

That's what the American staff member needed who gave me so many fits back in the beginning of our ministry in the former Soviet Union. He continued to suffer hardships after he left our organization. In the end, he discovered it wasn't conditions in the former USSR that were so difficult; it was his own outlook on life. I could have helped him overcome this problem much earlier, but he wasn't open to my help.

After a number of years in which he struggled from job to job and lived in personal misery because nothing ever satisfied him, this man finally came to understand that the problem wasn't the environment around him. The problem was deeper than that — it was rooted inside *himself*. The man began to make the needed adjustments, and today he is a viable member of the Body of Christ and a blessing to his church.

So remember — God knows how to change a person better than anyone else. Just because someone under your authority doesn't listen to you when you try to correct him doesn't mean he's a hopeless case. It may just mean that it isn't time for him to be spiritually promoted.

Perhaps he could submit better to another pastor or leader right now. Don't give up on him simply because of a bad experience. That wouldn't be the right thing to do. Love him, forgive him, and give him space to grow and learn some lessons about life.

The truth is, we've all been argumentative with those in authority over us at one time or another. We need to be careful not to judge others for the exact same thing we've done ourselves.

However, if you and a prospective candidate are not able to see eye to eye when you find it necessary to speak correction into his life, take it as a sure sign that you shouldn't proceed any further. There may come a time to take this relationship to a higher level within your leadership team, but that time is definitely not right now.

QUESTIONS FOR PERSONAL GROWTH OR GROUP DISCUSSION

1. What specific things should you look for in a person's behavior in order to determine how he or she responds to correction?

2. Explain Paul's main points of instruction regarding the correct way to give correction to those under you.

3. In a situation where someone under you has to be corrected, why isn't the question "Who is right or wrong?" the most important question to be answered?

4. Have you ever had anyone under your authority who strongly resisted correction? How did you deal with that person? What was the outcome of the situation?

5. What would you do differently today if you had to deal with a rebellious person under your authority?

NOTES:

_____

_____

_____

_____

_____

_____

_____

_____

_____

_____

_____

_____

_____

_____

_____

_____

_____

_____

_____

_____

_____

HAS THIS POTENTIAL LEADER BECOME ESSENTIAL TO YOU?

*N*ot long ago, I was preaching at our church on the subject of commitment to one's local church. Since I believe commitment to the Lord is reflected in the way a person serves his local church, I decided to ask the congregation some penetrating questions.

Many people in the congregation were visibly jarred as I asked:

- "In what ways are you *essential* to this church?"

- "What do you personally contribute that makes you indispensable to the way we operate?"

- "Would we feel your absence if you suddenly disappeared?"

- "Would anyone even know you were gone, except for the fact that your chair was empty?"

- "What is there about your contribution to the church that's so essential in a concrete way that we'd feel loss if you were no longer here?"

- "*Again I ask, are you essential to this church?*"

I heard moans and groans throughout the entire congregation. These questions really hit people right in the pit of their stomachs. One woman actually gasped so loudly that I could hear her on the stage where I was standing!

I heard another woman tell the lady sitting next to her, "I know the answer to that question! No one would miss me! I don't do a single thing in this church but sit right here in this chair week after week. Why would anyone miss me? I don't contribute anything!"

If a business leader is looking for someone to promote into a position of responsibility, whom does he consider for that promotion before anyone else? He looks to those who have been the most faithful, who have done the best job possible, and who have become so *essential* that the workplace has come to depend on them. A smart business leader would never take a nonactive, unknown person and put him into a position of leadership. That would be foolishness because the leader wouldn't be able to predict that person's work habits, level of productivity, or faithfulness to finish a job on time or as expected.

One of the marks of upcoming leaders is that they have already made themselves *essential* to the organization. You might say they have "stepped up to the plate," accepted responsibility, and filled a vacancy that desperately needed to be filled. Their diligence to do a job well has made them so crucial that the organization would suffer great loss if they suddenly disappeared. That's what I mean when I say they have made themselves *essential* to that organization.

When I think of the word "essential," I think of words such as *needed, required, crucial, central, key, necessary, mandatory, indispensable, imperative, urgent, meaningful, pivotal, unavoidable,* and *wanted.* When I'm looking for someone to fill a leadership vacancy in our ministry, I look to those who have made themselves meaningful, pivotal, and crucial — people who have become "key" to their various divisions and to Denise and me. *Why should we look to other pastures for leadership if we have such a leader right in front of us?*

> When I'm looking for someone to fill a leadership vacancy in our ministry, I look to those who have made themselves meaningful, pivotal, and crucial.

MY OWN ESSENTIAL LEADERS

I can give examples of people in our own organization who came to us as mere church members or entry-level staff members and later became essential to the growth and development of our ministry. Now these people hold key positions in our organization. In fact, they became so important to the operation of our ministry that Denise and I have come to lean heavily on them. Let me give you just a few examples — a mixture of different types of people — to demonstrate the point I'm making.

OUR ADMINISTRATOR

When our administrator in our organization first came to us some time ago, he had recently moved to Moscow from another nation to serve in the professional field. However, as time passed, he began to serve in various capacities of our church and organization. As he served, I could see that he was destined to become much more than a volunteer. We found him to be so faithful and dependable, so crucial to different aspects of our work, that soon we knew he was needed as a part of our team. I was impressed when I saw:

- His willingness to help in any capacity needed.

- His insights into problem-solving.

- His skills in working with and managing people.

- His outstanding and exceptional attitude.

All these points were like neon signs alerting me that this young man was to be a part of our staff. Now he has been on our team for so long and has performed so superbly that I can't imagine our organization operating without him. Of course, if he had to leave, God would provide his replacement. But I would hate to see him go because he has become such an essential part of our team.

If God called our administrator elsewhere, I know God would replace him with an equally capable person; however, Denise and I would feel a great loss if this good man left our ministry. His diligence, his commitment to thoroughly accomplishing his responsibilities, and his ability to carry out our God-given dreams and the vision of this ministry have made him *essential* to us personally and to the overall outreach of our ministry.

This staff member's pivotal role emerged *before* we gave him a position of authority. His abilities, his excellent attitude, and his willingness to serve in any capacity, even in menial tasks, eventually led to his appointment to this key position of leadership in our ministry.

MY EXECUTIVE ASSOCIATE PASTOR

The man who serves at my side in Moscow has been with me for many years. But as the years pass, I become more and more appreciative of him and what he does in our ministry. In fact, he has become such a pillar in our organization that I can truthfully say he has become a very essential part of our ministry.

When this individual first came into my life, I didn't fully recognize the great gift God had graciously brought to me. I had other associates who had been with me longer, so my tendency was to look to them instead of to him. As a result, I simply didn't see the full value of this man who had come alongside me in ministry.

But when we relocated to Moscow to start and establish the next phase of our work, it was this man who followed me and served at my side. The new situation forced us into a new kind of working relationship — and that is when I realized how crucial he was to become to our ministry.

Day by day I watched this person, becoming more and more impressed with the qualities he possessed in his life. These were qualities I highly esteem and aspire to in my own life and long to see in every leader who works at my side. Soon I realized that this man would be pivotal to the growth and expansion of our ministry. As I carefully watched and interacted with him, I came to see and value:

- His sound, dependable counsel and advice.

- His high regard for confidentiality.

- His desire to correctly represent me and not to represent himself.

- His willingness to serve long hours and to do it with a joyful heart.

- His readiness to tackle any assignment that I needed him to take.

- His love for God and love for people.

These attributes impressed me greatly, and as time passed, I found myself looking to him more and more. I was so blessed by this man and thanked God on a regular basis for bringing him and his wife to us so they could become a part of our team. Through the years, this leader has become extremely important to me. As a result, he now has a great deal of responsibility and authority in our ministry.

MY ASSOCIATE IN OUR ASSOCIATION OF PASTORS

When my associate in our large and ever-growing Pastors' Association first came to us, he was a young nineteen-year-old boy who had just graduated from the first above-ground Bible school in the USSR. At the time he first joined our team, I never would have dreamed he would hold the key position in our ministry that he does today. But because of his faithfulness through the years, this young man rose to a place of great responsibility in our organization. He became *essential* to me and *pivotal* to the overall operation of our ministry because of his many excellent qualities:

- His faithfulness to do a job well.

- His serious approach to the work of God.
- His view of ministry, which became identical to mine.
- His ability to communicate my heart.
- His commitment to me and to my vision.
- His representation of me to others.

All these qualities eventually made my associate absolutely essential and strategic to our ministry and to me personally. Of course, if he were suddenly gone, God would send us someone else to replace him. But initially I would feel a tremendous loss.

Because of the excellence with which this man served and carried out his various responsibilities alongside me through the years, it became obvious that he was the one to fill the associate position he holds today. But the point I'm making is that he demonstrated the characteristic of *leadership* long before he was given the title.

MY OFFICE MANAGER

When my office manager first came to our organization, she was a receptionist with minimal responsibilities. We didn't know her well, so we started giving her very small assignments to see how she worked and to determine her level of personal responsibility. It didn't take us too long to recognize the type of person she was — an eager-to-learn individual who had the inward makings to become a top-notch leader in our organization.

The test of time and experience proved that this woman was to be a key player in our ministry. I watched carefully as she:

- Worked laboriously for hours on end.

- Never complained about the workload that was put on her.

- Volunteered and jumped right in the middle of difficult projects to lend a helping hand.

- Stood by our sides and supported us in difficult and challenging moments.

As time passed, this staff member was advanced again and again to greater positions of responsibility. Today she is so dependable and crucial to our organization that I count her as one of our most important team members. The scope of her responsibilities in our organization today is massive. A list of what she is accountable for in our ministry would go on for pages.

When this woman first joined our staff years ago, I didn't know she would one day hold this powerful position of leadership on our team. But after a period of time, she became *essential* to us, and I knew we couldn't do without her.

THE DIRECTOR OF OUR TV MINISTRY

When our TV Director first came to us, he was young and inexperienced with television, but he had a fierce desire to learn and aspired for excellence in everything he did. Because he was so new to our organization, at first we didn't give him any key positions of leadership. To us, he was an unknown quantity, so I didn't feel comfortable about letting him do too much too quickly.

As time passed, I observed as he took his minimal responsibilities to heart and fulfilled all his tasks with great seriousness.

Both he and his wife were faithful to church and demonstrated a heart to serve, and I could see their deep love for God. After a while, it was impossible to ignore the fact that both he and his wife were emerging as leaders in our ministry. And I wasn't the only one who recognized this; others saw it too.

After a while, the former TV Director moved on to another position in another nation, and Denise and I had to choose a new leader for the television ministry. Some speculated about whom we would choose to replace the former TV Director, but there was never a doubt in our minds. No one could accuse us of moving hastily, for we had been watching this leader and his wife for many years. We knew how they reacted to various situations, and we had seen how they interrelated with other people. From years of observation, we knew this man:

- Was committed to the Lord.
- Was committed to our ministry.
- Was committed to Denise's and my leadership.
- Was committed to doing his work with professionalism.
- Was committed to imparting excellence to others.
- Was committed to being faithful in everything he set his hand to do.

When the time came for our former TV Director to leave, we knew this man was to step into that key leadership position. Years of observation and working with him gave us assurance that he would do the job well and in a manner that would please both the Lord and us.

After we put this man in charge of this department of our ministry, it wasn't long before the television ministry had become more highly organized than ever before and its scope of outreach had grown even larger. Today this man is *strategic* to what we are doing. If anyone can be depended on, Denise and I know it is he and his wife. Regardless of the need, the hour, or the work required, I know that this man can be called on and relied on as a key member of our team.

> People become leaders because they are no longer dispensable.

This staff member's actions, attitude, and willingness to serve made a place for him in our ministry. He became so *essential* that we eventually knew we didn't want to be without him. We felt he had become *imperative* to our ministry.

People become leaders because they are no longer *dispensable.* They become *needed.* They become *pivotal.* They fill a void that no one else is filling. They become a *reliable, steadfast,* and *needed* part of your team.

Therefore, as you look for people to join your top leadership team, it's wise to start with those who have made themselves *essential* to your organization.

OTHER LEADERS IN OUR ORGANIZATION

I could go on and on about the people who serve at our sides in all of our offices around the world. We have leaders who are talented, skilled, hard-working, and willing to make any sacrifices required to fulfill the vision God has assigned to us. They are simply the cream of the crop.

Others have come and gone through the years who were equally talented, but they did not have the inward makings to be a leader in our group. Although talented, other essential attributes were missing. As much as we valued their talent, their attitudes and work ethic did not align with ours; therefore, they never attained a top-level place of leadership in our organization.

Gifts and talents are great, but they are not everything when it comes to leadership. It is great if you can find a person who is talented, but most important are a potential leader's heart qualities. There are many gifted people who do not have the heart you need, are not willing to work the number of hours you will require of them, or have never demonstrated the kind of desire you need in leaders who serve at your side.

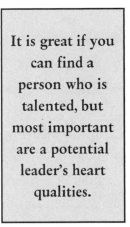

It is great if you can find a person who is talented, but most important are a potential leader's heart qualities.

(If you do not have copy of my book *If You Were God, Would You Choose You?* I encourage you to order a copy today. In this book, I discuss the role of gifts and talents versus the heart qualities that are most important to God. If you want to be used by God in a significant way, this is one book that you *must* read!)

Before you choose a leader, take a serious look at their lives and make sure you are selecting the right kind of person to serve on your team. You need to determine this person's potential value to your organization before you give him an important role on your team.

QUESTIONS TO ASK TO DETERMINE
SOMEONE'S VALUE TO AN ORGANIZATION

When I speak of determining a person's *value* to an organization, I'm not talking about his value as a human being. I'm referring to his value as a member of the team or the value of his contribution to the overall outreach and operation of the organization.

It's healthy for those who long to be leaders to pose thought-provoking questions to themselves that help them judge the true value of their contribution to the local church or ministry where God has called them.

Even though I am the senior pastor in our church and ministry, I regularly ask these kinds of questions to myself because I want to know if I'm effective or ineffective in the fulfilling of the vision God has given me. In the same way, it's prudent for *you* to take the time for self-evaluation — to be completely honest with yourself about who you are, what you are achieving, the attitudes you possess, and so on. Regardless of your present position, it would be healthy for you to honestly ask yourself:

- Am I contributing anything significant to my church?

- If I were gone, would anyone notice I was missing?

- Do I simply take from my church, or is there something concrete I'm imparting?

- Am I essential to the life of this organization?

- In what ways am I essential?

- Where am I serving and working in my home church?

- Am I a crucial part of the team?

- Do others view me as a team player on whom they can rely?

- Do people see me as a mere attendee of church services?

- Of what consequence am I to the local Body of Christ?

- Does the success of anything at this church depend on me?

- If I were someone else looking at me, would I think I'm a contributor to the well-being of the church — or just a person who attends meetings and asks for prayer when needed, but then goes home week after week, never really contributing anything concrete to the church?

Don't rush through these questions when you ask them to yourself. Take time to seriously consider the answers. It may also be interesting for you to go to a fellow worker or church member to see how he or she would answer these questions concerning your value on the team.

How we view ourselves is often not how others view us. Getting a second opinion is sometimes useful (and sometimes *painful*) in helping us ascertain what we are really contributing to the team.

There's nothing wrong with taking a good, honest look at ourselves to see how we can change and improve to become better than we currently are. These kinds of questions are penetrating enough that truthful answers should show where we fare well and where we need to do better.

When choosing leadership for our team, I apply these kinds of questions to each new candidate. If I take the time to think through each point — and if I lay aside my personal aspirations for that person so I can see a truthful picture — it helps me determine whether or not this potential leader is ready to step upward into a greater role of responsibility and authority.

MINISTRY IS *WORK*

Another thing that is extremely important to me is to know how a person works. So when I'm in the process of choosing someone to be a part of my leadership team, I want to know if this person knows how to work because *ministry is work*. Paul referred to it as *the work* of the ministry (Ephesians 4:12). Therefore, for a person to truly fulfill the responsibilities of ministry, he must maintain a serious attitude, he must be concentrated, focused, and completely committed. Sure, ministry can be done with a lesser commitment, but a lesser commitment produces lesser results — and I am not interested in lesser results!

In my book *If You Were God, Would You Choose You?* I go into great detail about the kind of expectations Jesus has for those who serve Him. Jesus made it very clear that He appreciates and rewards hard work. He also made it abundantly clear that He has little tolerance for those who are lazy and sluggish in their responsibilities. If this is Jesus' attitude toward work and responsibility, it must be my attitude as well.

When people come to work full-time on my staff, I want them to know what I expect of them. I expect them to act and carry on like committed, disciplined disciples who perform their responsibilities with excellence. I'm not interested in inviting people on my team whose entire commitment entails nothing more than attending church meetings and then immediately going home, never getting involved in the work of the church or the ministry.

Disciples are what I seek. I desire to develop and surround myself with people who are just as committed to doing the work of God as I am. As I look at people to determine their commitment level, I've found that a person's commitment level can *usually* be ascertained by his or her intensity of involvement in the ministry.

> I desire to develop and surround myself with people who are just as committed to doing the work of God as I am.

If someone tells me he wants to be a leader, yet he never shows up to help meet a need, *never* comes to a work day, never has time to do anything in the evenings because it inconveniences his family life, I know he is *not* the kind of leadership material I'm looking for to work alongside me.

LEADERSHIP IS NOT CONVENIENT

If your prospective leaders say your requirements are too much or too hard, *you have made another very valuable discovery*. They aren't willing to do what is required in terms of time and work in order to stand before people as leaders. It's better to know ahead of time that they aren't willing to pay the price you will expect of them later than to install them as leaders and then make this discovery.

Ask them to *prove* they are willing to pay the price connected to leadership. Give them work to do — and *lots* of it! When something needs to be done, call on them to do it, and expect them to do it with a happy heart. Leadership is serving — and if they're not willing to serve, they're not ready to be leaders.

If someone believes he is called to be a leader inside the church, then I expect him to act like a leader — and a leader is a

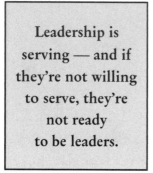

Leadership is serving — and if they're not willing to serve, they're not ready to be leaders.

person who gives himself to the work of the ministry. This includes all the needs, requests, and demands that accompany ministry.

Unfortunately, many people have a false impression about ministry. They imagine that ministry simply entails praying and reading their Bibles all day long. But ministry is much more than prayer and Bible study. It requires intense commitment to do the job well at any cost.

Whatever field you feel called to, you will never be successful by just putting half your heart into it. To succeed at your job, you must put your all into it. To succeed at your studies as a student, you must give yourself to your studies. To succeed as a spiritual leader in a church, ministry, or organization, you must take your role seriously and work as though the total success of that organization rises and falls on your actions.

Let me use the examples of churches and ministries for a moment to demonstrate my point. Through the years, I have preached in more than 2,500 different churches all over the world. When one has preached to that many different churches and has known that many different spiritual leaders, it becomes apparent what makes some people successful and what causes others to falter and fail.

As a rule, successful churches are led by people who know how to work and who are so committed to their vision that they give their whole lives to make it happen. It isn't just a job to them. It isn't just a position. *It's their entire life.* Everything they are, everything they do, everything they long to be and to fulfill is tied up in ministry God has entrusted to them. Therefore, they have a sense of responsibility and an urgency to get up, get moving, and make things happen.

Because hard work is required in order to achieve success, I never apologize for asking people to work. If they are *not* willing to lay down their lives for that position of leadership, they are not ready to be leaders.

Bringing a lazy, low-performing person into your team is one of the most frustrating experiences you'll ever have. This is especially true if *you're* a hard worker.

Jesus understood that ministry is hard work. He taught His disciples that working for God's Kingdom is all about serving others:

But it shall not be so among you: but whosoever will be great among you, let him be your minister; And whosoever will be chief among you, let him be

**your servant: Even as the Son of man came not to be
ministered unto, but to minister, and to give his life
a ransom for many.**

Matthew 20:26-28

Even Jesus didn't come to be served, but to serve and to give His life for many. Leadership is "giving one's life for many" just as Jesus did. A candidate must understand that if he agrees to step into a leadership position, he's agreeing to invest his life, energy, time, and heart into the people who are following him.

Therefore, let potential leaders step into a servant role and demonstrate that they want to give their lives for the vision God has given you for your church, ministry, or organization. Let them demonstrate this quality first; then you can slowly move them upwards into greater realms of authority.

When people are given authority too quickly, they don't appreciate the awesome responsibility they've been given. They also tend to think *too highly* of themselves. First Timothy 3:6 sternly warns against taking people too high too quickly.

A much wiser course is to take them upwards slowly while you watch how well they serve. This gives you the opportunity to observe what kind of attitude they maintain in the good times and the hard times.

Take enough time to accurately ascertain what kind of attitude your potential leaders possess. Don't worry that you might offend them by not promoting them faster. You're not conducting a popularity contest to make them want to be in leadership alongside you.

As the candidates serve, observe their attitude.

- Do they do it with joy?

- Do they do it begrudgingly?

- Are they happy to serve behind the scenes doing the less desirable tasks, even if they have already been doing it for a long time?

- Are they able to maintain a good attitude, even if they feel like it's time for someone else to step in for a while?

You see, we are all called to be servants. If we fail the test at this most basic level, there is nothing left to discuss. This is the most basic and elementary point for determining who is and who isn't qualified to be a part of your leadership.

LEADERS MUST UNDERSTAND THAT THEY'RE PART OF A TEAM

The apostle Paul told the Romans, "For I say, through the grace given unto me, to every man that is among you, not to think of himself more highly than he ought to think; but to think soberly, according as God hath dealt to every man the measure of faith" (Romans 12:3).

What a statement! If anyone could have thought highly of himself, it would have been Paul — *and he would have been correct!* Yet he admonishes us not to think too highly of ourselves, but to think "soberly."

The word "soberly" means *to be reasonable or sensible.* One Greek expositor says "soberly" means *to recognize your limits and respect them.* In other words, don't pretend to be more than you are! Recognize your God-given abilities and use them. But when you come to the edge of your limitations, realize that it's all right to say, "This is too much for me."

Leaders must understand that they're part of a team and then learn how to function in cooperation with others. No one can do it all alone.

If you try to act like you can do everything on your own, you're going to find it quite humiliating when you fail miserably in front of everyone. So instead of thinking too highly of yourself and attempting to go it alone with every project you undertake, develop a team mentality. Bring others into the project with you.

The Bible clearly teaches that there is safety among many counselors (Proverbs 11:14). Besides, no one is able to do everything perfectly.

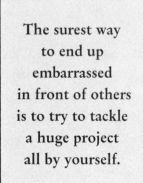

The surest way to end up embarrassed in front of others is to try to tackle a huge project all by yourself.

The surest way to end up embarrassed in front of others is to try to tackle a huge project all by yourself. When you fail and fall flat on your face, you'll regret that you didn't say, "I think someone else can do this job better than I can. This is simply not where I'm most gifted. Does anyone else on this team want to help me out with this project?"

When Paul said we were "...to think soberly, according as God hath dealt to every man the measure of faith," he was instructing us to remember that there are other members of the

Body of Christ too! We're not the only ones who are called and have faith. God has gifted His entire Body with faith and spiritual gifts. Therefore, rather than try to do it all, we are to think "soberly." *In other words, we're to recognize our limitations and allow other people to be used by God too!*

When those of us who are leaders follow this principle, it prevents us from thinking too highly of ourselves. Yes, we should respect the call of God on our lives; we should respect our ministry; and we should respect the position of responsibility God has given us. Our place of authority may place us in a more visible position than others, but, ultimately, we all need each other. We may hold different positions, but we are still members of the Body of Christ who are called to function corporately together.

KEEP THIS IN PERSPECTIVE

It's important as a leader to keep this in perspective. You may have a more visible position than others do during this earthly life, but your value to God for eternity is no different than anyone else in His Body.

People who are spiritually mature don't need to walk around talking about how "great" they are. Only on occasion did the apostle Paul talk about himself as being "great," and even then he didn't want to do it. He did it because of "false apostles" who were constantly trying to discredit his ministry.

In Second Corinthians 11, Paul finally forced himself to talk about all his own spiritual accomplishments. He hated talking about himself so much that he called it "foolishness." He just had to do it to fight the lies of those he called false apostles.

I get very concerned about a person who's always trying to "prove" how great and impressive he and his accomplishments are. It reveals an inner flaw that, if not corrected, could ultimately prove fatal to that person or to the ministry with which he works. Never forget that before Lucifer fell, he was very impressed with himself! It was this fatal flaw that ultimately brought him down.

When someone is always telling me or other members of my team how great he or she is, it's like a red flag that warns me something is seriously wrong with that person. According to Jesus, a "great" person is one who gets down on his hands and knees to serve other people (John 13:14,15) — *not* one who boasts about himself or makes himself look "great" in the eyes of others.

> According to Jesus, a "great" person is one who gets down on his hands and knees to serve other people.

Jesus said, "And whosoever of you will be the chiefest, shall be servant of all" (Mark 10:44). A "great" person's job is not to prove how great he is. According to Jesus, someone who is great in God's Kingdom is one who continually goes about the business of serving others.

Jesus continued by saying, "For even the Son of man came not to be ministered unto, but to minister, and to give his life a ransom for many" (Mark 10:45).

Think of it! Jesus is the Lord of all, the Creator of the Universe, the only begotten Son of God. Yet while He walked on this earth, He never once said to someone, "Excuse Me, but do you know how great I am? Do you realize that no one in the world is more anointed than I am?"

Of course, Jesus *was* great! In fact, no one was greater or more anointed than Jesus. Yet when He came, the Bible makes it clear that his primary objectives were "...to minister, and to give his life a ransom for many" (Matthew 20:28). Jesus' primary purpose was to serve and to give His life away, not to be served or to demand the adoration of men.

Certainly we should respect the spiritual gifts and offices God has given to the Body of Christ. For example, a pastor should be respected and held in honor because of the position God has given him. Pastors hold incredible positions of authority and will give account to God for how they have handled their pastoral responsibilities. Because they teach the Word of God, the Bible says they will be judged more strictly (James 3:1).

Anyone who stands in a ministry position will one day answer to the One who called him or her. But so will the person who serves as a greeter at the door of the church. So will the person who works in the nursery. So will the person who is called by God to vacuum and clean the church building. Those whom God has called to fill each of these positions will be accountable to Him for the way they did or did not do their job.

Of course, greeters and nursery workers can be more easily replaced than a pastor, and they don't carry the same level of responsibility or authority that a pastor carries. But that doesn't mean these positions are not important. Every person who holds responsibility in the local church is vital to its growth and life.

This is why it is so vital that people see their leaders' willingness to come down to their level and identify with them, live with them, walk with them, pray with them, and lead them by example. As Paul told the Thessalonians, "So being affectionately desirous of you, we were willing to have imparted unto you, not the gospel of God only, but also our own souls because ye were dear unto us" (1 Thessalonians 2:8).

Paul loved the Thessalonians so fervently that he was willing to give them not only the Gospel, but his very life as well. What a package he offered them! He gave them the Word, and he gave them his life. Nothing beats that kind of deal. Nothing is more effective than a leader who preaches the Word and then climbs down into the pit with his people in order to lead them, teach them, and help them climb up to higher ground.

> Nothing is more effective than a leader who preaches the Word and then climbs down into the pit with his people in order to lead them, teach them, and help them climb up to higher ground.

Think how spiritually mature Paul must have been! He was truly a great man, yet he laid aside all his own accomplishments and fame to climb down to where the people were. He was so secure in who he was in Jesus Christ that he didn't need to demand any special recognition from those to whom he ministered.

Besides, Paul knew that someday when he stood before the Lord with other believers, he wouldn't receive any special treatment. He would be just another believer who had received the call of God and tried to be faithful. He would be just like everyone else in the Body of Christ.

STEADFAST, IMMOVABLE, ALWAYS ABOUNDING
IN THE WORK OF THE LORD

In First Corinthians 15:58, Paul wrote, "Therefore, my beloved brethren, be ye stedfast, unmoveable, always abounding in the work of the Lord...." What does it mean to be *steadfast* and *immovable?*

The word "steadfast" has several meanings:

- It means to be *stationary*, such as *something that sits in one place for a long, long time.*

- It also describes *something that is firm and steady.*

- It was frequently used in connection with *foundations or support structures in buildings.*

- It describes *something that is strong, unbendable, unbreakable and permanent,* such as a well-built foundation for a large building or a strong column that holds up a roof.

So when Paul urges us to be "steadfast," he's calling on us to be totally reliable — not shaky or undependable. We should be *stationary* in our roles in the Body of Christ. We shouldn't be quickly shaken nor easily lured to some other place or some other task. We must be like *pillars, foundations,* or *supports* in the house of God.

When you see a huge stone pillar in a building, what is its purpose? It's supporting the roof or some other important part of the building, correct? If you were to suddenly jerk that pillar out of its place, what would happen to the building? It would fall down and create a horrible, terrible mess! The whole building would collapse into a heap of rubble.

What would happen if you built a large building without a foundation? That building might look cosmetically beautiful. But when the weather grew cold and the ground swelled from frost heave, that building would quickly begin to lean this way and that way. Eventually, there wouldn't be enough support underneath it to hold the building in place. It would literally come apart at its seams!

When you build an extremely large building, the foundation must be bigger and stronger than normal. The weight of a giant structure demands a larger foundation. If the foundation isn't large enough or strong enough for that big building to sit on, it will crack and move, causing irreparable structural problems that make the building unsafe for occupancy.

Likewise, the Church of Jesus Christ must have a good foundation if it is going to endure throughout the ages. Our primary foundation is the Lordship of Jesus Christ (1 Corinthians 3:11). But the same text tells us that once the foundation of Jesus' Lordship has been laid, we must be very careful how we continue to build on top of it! *(See* 1 Corinthians 3:12-15.)

If you act as though you're building something that has to last only a few years, you'll settle for a shabby structure that isn't built very well. But when your goal is to build the Body of Christ to endure for ages to come, you necessarily become more careful and quality-minded about the manner in which you build. You will seek to use good materials; you'll take time in mixing them together properly; and you'll tediously put them in their proper places.

> Hasty building
> produces shaky
> structures. Careful
> and cautious
> building produces
> strong, steady
> structures.

Hasty building produces shaky structures. Careful and cautious building produces strong, steady structures.

This is why we must be so careful as we select leaders and lay hands on people for positions of authority. We must view the Church as something that will last for ages to come; hence, we must use the most faithful, solid, and committed people we can find, making certain that they're trained and ready before we put them in positions of responsibility.

One of the worst scenarios that can happen in the selection of leadership is to place people in key positions, only to have them pull out at a dreadful moment. When this occurs, there is suddenly a giant gap in the Church. A place of support has been vacated, causing all kinds of problems to erupt. That's why potential leaders should be tested and proven faithful before they're placed in positions of responsibility.

> Once you know
> the place God has
> called you to serve,
> you must begin to
> look at yourself
> as a "pillar" or
> as part of the
> "foundation" of
> the Church.

Once a leader is in place, you can't afford for him to suddenly change his mind and pull out of that position. That kind of sudden change negatively affects too many lives. The welfare of the Body of Christ is too serious a matter to make this kind of mistake.

This is why Paul urges you to be "steadfast." In other words, once you know the place God has called you to serve, you must begin to look at yourself as a "pillar" or as part of the "found-ation" of the Church.

Don't view yourself as small and insignificant. You are part of the foundation of the Body of Christ! You are one of the pillars! If you're thinking differently than this, then you're wrong and you need to change your thinking.

STEADFAST AND *IMMOVABLE*

According to Paul, you must also be "immovable." The word "immovable" in Greek means *not capable of being moved from one place to another place.* In other words, once you've said yes to the call of God, you should be a *permanent fixture* in the house of God!

Something that is immovable is also:

- Rock Solid
- Fixed
- Solid
- Grounded
- Established
- Rooted

- Cemented
- Glued
- Anchored
- Unvarying
- Permanent
- Stable

When a person knows that God has called him to do something, he must develop that kind of rock-solid, immovable attitude about that task or project because it is certain that Satan will attempt to sidetrack anyone whom God calls to do a job. The devil will try to use people, finances, circumstances, discouragement, and a host of other tactics to move someone off course from his intended goal.

This makes it even more imperative that a leader would make up his mind to be fixed, rooted, grounded, anchored, and unvarying in his commitment to accomplish the task God has set before him. Likewise, the leader must recognize that he is an example to the rest of the flock. If he is inconsistent and wavering in his commitment, he sets a bad example for those who follow him. Those under his care or supervision need to see that he is consistent and committed to do his job correctly, regardless of what it costs him.

For a leader to be effective, he must be thoroughly dedicated to do his job; he must stick with his job; and he must carry through until his job is done the way the Lord and his pastor, boss, or supervisor expects it to be done. Nothing less should be satisfactory to someone who desires a leadership position.

When I look for people to serve in key leadership roles in our church, I want to see if they demonstrate these characteristics of leadership. I realize that whatever qualities they possess is exactly what they will impart to their particular area of responsibility or ministry. If they demonstrate stability and faithful endurance in what they do, this is *precisely* the spirit of excellence and commitment they will impart to their entire division of the ministry.

This is why the apostle Paul urges us to be immovable in our commitment to the work of the Lord. Then he goes on to tell us *how much* we should be involved in service to God's Kingdom. He says that we should be *"abounding* in the work of the Lord."

Notice that Paul refers to "the *work* of the Lord." Once again, he confirms to us that ministry is not sitting on the sidelines and watching; rather, ministry is *work*. To fulfill one's responsibilities in ministry effectively and successfully requires a person's fullest attention. If a person is inactive, easygoing, slow-moving, or casual in his approach to ministry, he will probably never build anything significant in his particular realm of responsibility.

Therefore, I want to know if a potential leader and I are compatible regarding this subject of work. Do we have the same kind of work ethic, or will we find ourselves on different sides of the line on this issue? Is the candidate someone who watches the clock and punches his time card exactly when the minute hand strikes at closing time, or is he a person who is committed to getting the job done correctly, regardless of the hours he might need to devote to his assignment?

I understand that staff and church workers have responsibilities at home too. I'm also a husband and father. I know that for me to live responsibly before God, I must succeed first with my family. So when a person tries to protect his time with his family, I consider this quality commendable and right.

However, there are times when the ministry just isn't convenient. During these times, leaders must do what they must do in order to finish a job or an assignment. Therefore, if a potential leader is never willing to put in extra hours and he never stays late to work with the rest of the team in order to get a job done, then I know this person will never fit into our group. He isn't the kind of team player I'm looking for to be a part of our top leadership.

So before I take a person into higher realms of responsibility and authority, I take time to watch and see what kind of worker he is. I ask:

- Is he is a constant clock-watcher?

- Do his work habits demonstrate that he loves the ministry and wants to invest in it?

- How involved in the work of the ministry is this potential leader right now — before we give him a higher level of leadership responsibilities?

- Does this potential leader show by his actions that he is abounding in the work of the Lord?

- Does he display a servant mentality, or do we have to beg and plead with him to participate?

- Can I depend on this person, or will I feel like "I'm left holding the bag alone" if I bring him into my team?

After I pose these questions to myself, I then bring my top leadership team together to see what they know about this potential leader. Since he will be working alongside them, I believe it's vital for them to tell me what they know.

Occasionally, my view of a potential leader has been blurred or inaccurate. You see, my responsibility is to oversee the entire ministry, so at times I haven't been close enough to determine the exact facts pertaining to a potential leader. From a distance that person may look good — *very good* — to my eyes. But sometimes those who work closely with a candidate I'm considering for leadership have a totally different view. They've "rubbed shoulders" on a daily basis with that person, so they may be aware of things I can't see.

Because I value my staff members' opinions, I ask them what they think. I want to know what they perceive about this person's attitude, character, and willingness to work. I ask them whether the candidate has given us any cause *not* to promote him at this time.

Listening to my team members' opinions not only helps me — it also lets them know that their input is important to me. It pulls them into the decision-making process and conveys how much I value them as part of my team. It also gives me a sure footing in my final decision because they have helped me make the decision and therefore share a sense of responsibility about that decision with me.

So I ask my staff:

- Who knows what kind of worker this potential leader is?

- Has he ever demonstrated any cause for concern that I should know about?

- Is there any reason you wouldn't put him into a higher leadership role?

- What kind of work ethic does he possess?

- Is he is a clock-watcher?

- Do you find that he willingly volunteers, or do you have to beg him to serve?

- What kind of work does he produce?

- Does he have any problems at home that affect his ability to serve?

I'm looking for people who are "abounding in the work of the Lord" — not people who do just the minimum amount required and then head for the door. Doing the minimum never builds a strong church, ministry, business, or organization.

If you want to build a strong, powerful, effective organization that impacts the world for the Gospel's sake, you must first build a leadership team in which every member is willing to do the maximum. In other words, the entire team gives their utmost, highest, supreme attention to their responsibilities. As a result of this "maximum mentality," the team produces top-notch results that you can feel good about in the Presence of the Lord.

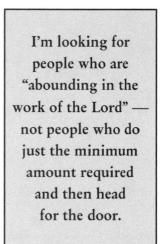

I'm looking for people who are "abounding in the work of the Lord" — not people who do just the minimum amount required and then head for the door.

Always remember — this isn't *our* work we're doing; it's "the work of *the Lord.*" *No* work we do is more important than what we do in His name.

When a person gives his utmost effort to his work, it won't be too long before his area of ministry will start growing superbly. As long as his actions are consistent and he diligently sticks with his assignment for a continuous period of time, his division of the ministry will grow.

When that person's division does start expanding and multiplying, you won't have to look for a new leader to take charge of the greater responsibilities. You'll realize that the leader who is presently in charge is the person you need. By being faithful and diligent, this leader has made himself *essential* to you and to your church, ministry, or organization.

So when you're choosing leadership for your team, be sure to ask: *Has this potential leader made himself essential to me and to our organization?* Your answer to this question may tell you whether or not this person is ready for a spiritual promotion.

QUESTIONS FOR PERSONAL GROWTH OR GROUP DISCUSSION

1. When you look at your own role in your local church, can you honestly say that your contribution has made you essential to that body of believers?

2. How can you use time and experience to help you determine whether or not a prospective leader will make an essential contribution to your church, ministry, or organization?

3. What outward signs indicate a person's level of commitment to the work of the ministry?

4. What specific qualities provide the external proof that a person is "always abounding in the work of the Lord"?

5. Think of someone in your life whom you consider essential to the fulfilling of your God-ordained purpose on this earth. What qualities does this person possess that make him or her essential?

NOTES:

_____

_____

_____

_____

_____

_____

_____

_____

_____

_____

_____

_____

_____

_____

_____

_____

_____

_____

_____

_____

_____

_____

IF THE CANDIDATE HAS COME FROM ANOTHER CHURCH, FIND OUT WHY

*P*eople change churches all the time, claiming different reasons why they left this church and that church or why they feel God is calling them here or there. Be very careful of people who join your church after having been members of various other churches. They'll *probably* leave you too.

I don't want to sound too emphatic on this point, but I've found that this is usually the case. Thousands of pastors all over the world could also testify about people who habitually leave churches to try out other churches.

Honestly, if church-hoppers come to our church, I'm glad they're there and I try to give them solid teaching from God's Word that will make a big difference in their lives. But I don't consider them to really be part of our congregation until they have demonstrated their consistency and faithfulness to me. I especially watch to see how they respond to conflict. Can they submit to spiritual authority, or are they going to run off as soon as they reach one of those "make-or-break" points in their relationship with me and our church?

When people float from church to church, they are usually seeking something they haven't found yet. *It may be that they are sincerely seeking better teaching or a deeper experience in worship.* This can especially be true when people have just recently gotten saved. They may need time to discover what kind of congregation they feel most comfortable in, or they may need a little extra time to discern exactly where the Lord wants them to attend church.

A believer's inability to settle in and commit to a local church is often a sign of a problem in his spiritual walk. You see,

> A believer's inability to settle in and commit to a local church is often a sign of a problem in his spiritual walk.

it's normal for people to take time to find the right church when they're new believers or when they've just moved to a new city. But something is drastically wrong when they have been believers for a long time or have lived in a particular location for a number of years but still can't find a church where they can serve.

Every believer should be able to find a church where he can serve the Lord. Even if it's not an ideal situation, there should be some kind of church where he can settle down to raise his family, use his gifts and talents to serve others, and be faithful in God's house.

I'm concerned that some people are too picky in the way they look for a church. They seem to be seeking something that doesn't exist anywhere on planet earth. You see, even the best churches are started and led by imperfect people. As long as people are in the church, it will have mistakes, flaws, occasional hang-ups, inconsistencies, and other problems connected to human beings. Unfortunately, there is no way around this fact of life.

'SUPER-SPIRITUALS' ARE OFTEN THE MOST DIFFICULT PEOPLE

I'll never forget an experience I had with some "floaters" many years ago. One night after I had finished ministering in a particular church, a man and his wife approached me. This couple said to me, "We see that you have a strong anointing on your life. We came here tonight so you could give us a word from the Lord."

To my surprise, they pushed the record button on a small handheld tape recorder, held it up to my mouth, and waited for me to give them a prophecy "on demand." They looked at me, just waiting for a prophecy they could record and take home with them that night.

I asked the couple, "What church do you attend in this city?"

"We haven't been able to find a church in this city," they answered. "We've looked and looked, but we've never found one that meets our criteria."

"How long have you lived here?" I asked.

"Fifteen years, and we've been trying to find a church where we could fit in the entire time," they replied.

When I heard that this couple had lived in that town fifteen years and had never found a church where they could serve, I was *shocked*! I personally knew five pastors in that city who had great churches.

The couple's answer let me know that they were spiritual dissidents who most likely lived under a facade of a false spirituality. That's why they had never connected to a church.

I felt an urgency to respond to what they had just requested of me, so I told them, "Put that microphone right up to my mouth. I'm sensing a strong word from the Lord for you tonight."

With anticipation they waited. I looked into their eyes and said, *"Thus saith the Lord: Repent of your stubborn and rebellious heart, and go join yourself to a pastor and to a local church!"*

They had expected a prophetic word that would take them up to the outer atmosphere. But they didn't need a word that took them out farther — *they needed a word that would bring them back down to earth!* They needed someone to rebuke them and tell them to learn to serve and be faithful in a local church.

UNSTABLE PEOPLE ARE UNPROFITABLE PEOPLE

All over the world, I hear pastors and church leaders relate their own examples of dealing with people who are so "spiritual" that no church can please them. Denise and I had a couple of people like this in the early days of our marriage when we were pastoring our first church.

Two ladies came to our church who had what we thought was a deep view of the Word and a deep spirituality. However, both women had attended five other churches *before* they came to our church. We were the *sixth church* they had attended in five years. I knew this wasn't a good sign.

The women told me, "Pastor Rick, we feel the Lord is leading us to become a part of your church. When we hear you speak, we know you have a spiritual level that is right for us."

These two ladies had wonderful personalities, and Denise and I enjoyed talking with them and hearing some of their insights into the Word. On several occasions, I even preached on a few of the insights they had shared with me.

But these ladies had never settled down into one church and stayed there. Because they had vacillated from one place to another for so many years, other pastors laughed when they heard the women were now attending our church. The pastors told us "Now it's your turn! They've already been everywhere else!"

I longed for these women to break the habit of being first *"called to"* and then *"called away"* from church after church. But they had been in the routine of changing churches for so long, I knew it would be difficult for them to break this chronic pattern. They had also made such a reputation for themselves of being unstable that no pastor or church in town took them seriously — even though they really possessed some awesome insights that would have benefited a local congregation. The "Lord" had simply led these ladies *to* and *from* too many churches.

But the truth was, the Lord couldn't have been leading those women. Their behavior was too erratic to be attributed to the leading of the Lord. If it had been the Lord, it was making Him look like He didn't know *what* He wanted those ladies to do!

A SURE SIGN OF SPIRITUAL PROBLEMS

When someone has a chronic pattern of moving from one church to another, you can be 99% sure that this person has some type of spiritual problem. If you talk to him, he will probably tell you why *none* of those churches was good enough. But all the churches in a city can't be wrong.

Be aware that a person who can't find a church good enough for him probably won't be pleased with your church either. Something is very wrong spiritually with this type of person.

I've discovered through the years that people who continually move from church to church are frequently judgmental, critical of leadership, and unwilling to submit to spiritual authority. That's why they never stay in one church very long.

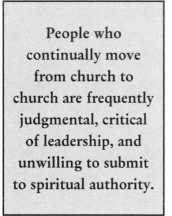

People who continually move from church to church are frequently judgmental, critical of leadership, and unwilling to submit to spiritual authority.

As in the case given above, these "floaters" frequently tell the pastor, *"I love you. You are the best pastor in the city. I thank God for your ministry."* They may even do fine in the church as long as the pastor doesn't talk about subjects such as *tithing, submission, authority, commitment,* or *money.* But as soon as the pastor touches on a subject that these people consider to be unspiritual or that rubs them the wrong way, they are out of that church and on their way to the next. One week earlier they loved the pastor. But now they are judging him as they walk out the door.

How do I know this so well?

Because unfortunately, the Body of Christ is filled with these kinds of people. Regardless of where you live, people who float from church to church will eventually find the path to your church as well — if they haven't already. You'll recognize them by their rebellion to authority, which is usually disguised under a mask of super-spirituality.

I'm not being unkind or too hard. This is the voice of experience speaking to you right now!

Let me give you this recommendation: When a person comes to you from another church, don't use him at first. Even if you think his potential is great, first let him *prove* that he is really called to your church and submitted to your authority.

Tell him to sit under the Word for a while before he gets involved so he can know you and your heart better. If he is really so *spiritual,* he should be able to recognize this as wise counsel.

But suppose he gets frustrated, upset, and tired of sitting. Suppose he throws up his arms in the air and says, "I'm out of here! I'm tired of waiting to be used!" In that case, just let him go. That kind of fleshly response reveals the truth about whether or not God called him to your church.

If God really called him to your church, he should be happy to sit there for the next thousand years if that's what you ask him to do. But when his commitment to you and your church is determined by whether or not he's allowed to sing, teach a Sunday school class, or hold any kind of responsible position, you are better off *to let him go.*

Should he choose to leave, don't chase after him and beg him to come back. If he were really called to be with you, you

> It's better to know who people are before you give them authority than to discover problems later.

couldn't *chase* him away. This is an excellent test to find out why that person has come to your church and why he wants to be one of your leaders.

It's better to know who people are *before* you give them authority than to discover problems later. So when you are about to lay your hands on someone, don't make the mistake of moving too fast.

Know that person. Know his character. Know his attitude. Know his good points. Know his weak points. Before you lay your hands on him and give him your seal of approval, *know* him!

FIVE KEY WORDS TO REMEMBER WHEN TESTING POTENTIAL LEADERS

I want to recommend a simple method to help you test to see if newcomers to your church or ministry are ready to be a part of your leadership team. I've applied these points in my own ministry and have found them to be very helpful.

For me, it's very important to know that I'm dealing with potential leaders who will keep their commitments. And if they have come from a number of other churches, I especially want to be assured that this time their commitment is going to stick.

If a newcomer has demonstrated instability in the past, I suggest that you *first test his character* before giving him a permanent position of authority. What do I mean by *test* him?

Well, the word *test* means to *investigate, inspect, experiment, analyze, and put on probation.*

I'm going to discuss each of these five words as a separate point. You'll see what I mean when I say that you should test the potential leader. Let these five words be your guide as you begin to seriously consider a new person for leadership in your church or organization.

INVESTIGATE

Before you give that person a permanent position of authority, *first investigate him.* If he has come to your church or organization from another church or organization, find out *why* he left the last place. Call the other pastor or leader and ask if he has any pertinent information about the candidate that you ought to know.

If the candidate was a problem in that former setting, the pastor or leader will be grateful for the opportunity to tell you the truth and protect you from what harmed him. So take the time to investigate before making a final decision!

INSPECT

Carefully inspect the potential leader's life and work. Give him small things to do; then follow up to see how he fulfilled his assignments. Did he do what you asked? Did he do it on time? Was he able to take orders and follow directions?

How about his personal life? Everything that glitters isn't gold, and everything newcomers want you to see isn't necessarily the truth. Does the candidate have harmony in his marriage? Are his children submissive and respectful to authority?

EXPERIMENT

Experiment by giving that person various levels of responsibility to see how he performs. Watch to see if he shows up on time or if he's regularly late. See how he does under pressure. How does he function in conflict situations? Does he take sides? Does he stay neutral?

Does the candidate pray and demonstrate a life of faith? Does he faithfully give tithes and offerings to the church or ministry? Is he sacrificing the way a leader should sacrifice? If you ask him to do something he has never done before, is he willing to try, to learn, and to develop himself? Or is he hesitant, unwilling, and unbendable?

It is very important that you know *whom* you are inviting into your team of leaders. You shouldn't invite an unknown factor into your midst who might disturb the peaceful agreement and unity you have worked so hard to build between you and your leaders.

ANALYZE

Once you've *investigated* who the candidates are, *inspected* how they work and live, and *experimented* by giving them small amounts of responsibility, it's time for you to make an *analysis*.

As pastor or leader of your ministry or organization, you are the one who must make the final call on whether or not a candidate qualifies to be a leader. To help you make that crucial decision, you must study all the information you have accumulated and prayerfully ask God to help you see the truth.

Play it on the safe side. Once you've concluded that this person is usable, it's still best to refrain from making a grand announcement about his new promotion in your church or organization. Before you do that, *first put him on probation.*

PROBATION

Even when a young man and woman consider each other to be physically attractive, that isn't a good enough reason for them to get married. Marriage is too serious to be based on looks alone. Likewise, your leadership team is too important to "marry itself" to someone just because the candidate seems to be a good match with the current team members.

Make sure you really want that new person. Be certain you're really *made for each other* before you "tie the knot."

This cautious approach is better for everyone involved. It may be that the potential leader mistakenly believes that he *wants* to be a leader. Later after the new working relationship is initiated, he may discover your method of leadership isn't compatible with his ability to follow. That's why it's better to wait and be sure both parties are really certain about making the commitment than it is to enter into a "marriage" that doesn't last.

Therefore, *put him on trial for three to six months.* If he is meant to be a part of your leadership team, he'll be happy to wait. If he isn't willing to undergo a time of testing, then you already have a good indicator that he'll have a problem submitting to your authority in the future.

I'm going to make a statement of fact that is *guaranteed* to be true: At some point in the future, every leader on your team will have an occasion to disagree with you. You *will* encounter opportunities for conflict. You will see something one way, and the leader will see it another way.

Disagreement is just a part of life. So no matter how peaceable and kind a potential leader seems right now, just expect it to happen at some point in the future.

Given the inevitability of disagreement, it's far better to find out how the potential leader handles conflict and disagreement *before* you've established him in a highly visible position of leadership. If you discover this person can't handle conflict, it's better not to use him as a leader. If he doesn't have the maturity to disagree and walk in unity at the same time, he isn't mature enough yet to stand in a position of leadership.

> You can't know what a person will do unless you allow a situation to arise that exposes his weaknesses and strengths.

Unfortunately, you can't know what a person will do unless you allow a situation to arise that exposes his weaknesses and strengths. That's why a time of probation is so valuable. It's a whole lot harder to get someone *out* of power than it is to take the extra time to know him, test him, and discover his weaknesses *before* you give him power.

When you act too quickly, you may find yourself dragged into a very uncomfortable situation in which you have to get someone out of a position *you* placed him in. It's a sad and messy dilemma — but you're the guilty one because *you're* the one who did it!

This cautious approach to selecting leadership may take a little longer, but what it saves you in tears, sorrow, and pain is well worth it. If you follow this approach, you'll feel better about your choices for leadership because you'll know the candidates' hearts and the attitude they project in life.

When you present them to your congregation or organization, you'll feel like you're standing on solid ground because you've done your homework. Most importantly, you'll be spared the pain of putting people into leadership who look good but whose hearts are not with you.

QUESTIONS FOR PERSONAL GROWTH OR GROUP DISCUSSION

1. What kind of spiritual problems may lie behind a person's inability to settle in and commit to a local church?

2. In what way might those same spiritual problems affect that person's ability to lead in your church, ministry, or organization?

3. What five steps should you take to test and evaluate a newcomer's ability to lead?

4. Why is a time of probation so valuable in determining a prospective candidate's ability to lead?

5. What qualities should be demonstrated by a member of your church or organization before you consider that person an integral part of the vision God has placed on your heart to fulfill?

NOTES:

_____

_____

_____

_____

_____

_____

_____

_____

_____

_____

_____

_____

_____

_____

_____

_____

_____

_____

_____

_____

_____

DOES THE PROSPECTIVE LEADER GIVE TITHES AND OFFERINGS?

*W*hat a person does with his money tells a lot about his priorities in life. Jesus said, "For where your treasure is, there will your heart be also" (Matthew 6:21).

Jesus' teaching is very clear: *What a person does with his money reveals what is inside his heart.* For example, someone may say he loves the local church. But if he never gives one cent to the church, the principle stated in Matthew 6:21 says his heart is *not* in the church, no matter *what* he says. *Where is his treasure?* If his treasure isn't in the church, his heart isn't in the church either.

I may say I love the Lord, but if I don't tithe as the Lord commands, what does it say about me? I'm either ignorant about tithing, or my words are cheap. If I really loved the Lord, *my money would reflect that I love Him.* I would *tithe.*

Words are cheap and easily spoken. Anyone can say he loves his church. But when a person sacrifices and gives to the church he is demonstrating that his words are *real.* His heart really is *in* the church.

If a person *never* gives to the church, it reveals that he either has no money or that he's a liar. Of course, a person who has no money will find it difficult to give. But if he *does* have money and *doesn't* give, his words and actions don't match. When he spends his extra money on all kinds of material junk and then drops a few dollars into the offering, he's telling the *true* story! He loves his junk more than he loves the church.

MONEY TELLS THE TRUTH!

Consider a man who says he loves his wife but never gives her any money or special gifts to demonstrate that love. Yet somehow that same man is able to find the money to go fishing, buy a fishing boat, go work out at the gym with the guys, and so on. What has he demonstrated? *He loves himself more than he loves his wife.* That's why he's spending his treasure on himself.

How many men have told their wives, "I love you, Sweetheart" and then spent all their extra money on themselves? Then the wife is told that there just isn't any money available to do what *she* wants to do.

> Jesus made it very clear that where a person's treasure is — where his money is — that's where his heart will be also.

How does it make the wife feel when her husband does this to her time after time? He can say, "I love you" all he wants, but she knows he really loves *himself.* What he does with his money tells the *real* story.

Jesus made it very clear that where a person's treasure is — where his *money is* — that's where his heart will be also. So if you want to know where a person's heart is, *follow his money* and you'll find out. Again I say, *money tells the truth!*

Does your potential leader spend most of his money on entertainment? Does he spend it on television sets and VCRs? Does he put it in the bank and save it for himself? Does he give most of his most of his money to the work of the Gospel?

Let me look at a person's finances, and in just a matter of minutes I can tell you what the most important thing is in his life. *The way he spends his money will tell the whole story of what he prizes, cherishes, loves, and adores.*

Of course, everyone has basic needs of life that require money, such as food, electricity, gas for the car, and so on. But once these things are paid, what a person does with the money that's left over will tell you what he esteems more highly than anything else.

God wants to bless His people with all kinds of material possessions. But He requires that His Kingdom always has first place in our lives, even with our finances (Matthew 6:33).

This may sound like a very narrow teaching about money, but years of experience with people has proven to me again and again that the words of Jesus are true. Follow a person's money, and you'll discover what *is* or *isn't* important to that person's life.

Two Questions To Ask

Before any person becomes a leader in our church, I first ask him two important questions:

- Do you tithe?

- Do you give special, additional offerings to the church?

I'm *not* after that person's money; I'm after his *heart*. His honest answers to these two questions tell me what I need to know about how committed he really is to the church.

Even if he has great potential and is loaded with talent — even if he has the right "look" for leadership and a special ability to communicate and lead — he cannot be a leader in our church if he doesn't tithe and give special offerings. His lack of giving proves that his heart is not as solidly fixed in the church as it ought to be to qualify as a leader.

A pastor should never apologize for asking a potential leader if he tithes and gives special offerings to the church. If that person responds by saying it's a private matter between him and God and not any of the pastor's business, he is *wrong*!

> Where a person spends his money tells the truth about what he values most highly in life.

You don't need to know *how much* money the prospective leader earns unless he chooses to tell you. You also don't need to know the *amount* he gives in his tithes and offerings. But in order to determine whether or not he is really committed to the church, you *do* need to know if he gives. It's your business to know, and you need never apologize for asking. How the person gives or doesn't give provides you with much-needed insight into his heart.

So remember, *where a person spends his money tells the truth about what he values most highly in life.*

QUESTIONS FOR PERSONAL GROWTH OR GROUP DISCUSSION

1. Jesus said, "For where your treasure is, there will your heart be also" (Matthew 6:21). In what specific ways can you act on the truth of this scripture in order to locate the heart of a potential leader?

2. What are the two questions to ask to find out what a potential leader values the most?

3. How do you reconcile these two truths in your own life and in the lives of your prospective leaders? 1) God wants His people to enjoy material possessions in this life; and 2) He wants His people to be joyful and generous givers.

4. What should be your response if a potential leader refuses to disclose his tithing and giving practices?

NOTES:

_____

_____

_____

_____

_____

_____

_____

_____

_____

_____

_____

_____

_____

_____

_____

_____

_____

_____

_____

_____

DOES THIS POTENTIAL LEADER HAVE A HEALTHY SPIRITUAL LIFE?

*W*e've looked at nine very important guidelines for determining who is and who is not ready for spiritual promotion. However, one very important question remains: *Does the potential leader have a healthy spiritual life?*

I have frequently been amazed by how many people serve every Sunday in church but have little or no private, personal time with the Lord. *They serve the Lord, but they really don't know Him intimately.*

But when you serve in a leadership capacity in the church, an intimate relationship with the Lord is not an option. You cannot spiritually help people if you don't draw from a regular source of spiritual fellowship with the Lord yourself. You may be able to draw from the spiritual reserves within you for a while, but eventually you'll run out of steam and feel like you have nothing more to give.

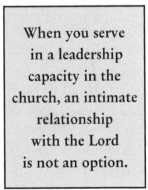

When you serve in a leadership capacity in the church, an intimate relationship with the Lord is not an option.

A CANDIDATE'S PRIVATE SPIRITUAL LIFE AFFECTS
HIS ANOINTING FOR MINISTRY

This is why a leader must constantly keep his spiritual life intact — so he himself is refreshed and filled with the life and the power of God to minister to others. It isn't possible for a leader to tell others about One with whom he has no fresh, living relationship. Therefore, maintaining an intimate relationship with the Lord is *obligatory* for those who stand in any kind of spiritual leadership position.

> It isn't possible for a leader to tell others about One with whom he has no fresh, living relationship.

For instance, how can an usher or greeter impart joy to people as they enter the church if he or she never spends time in the Presence of the Lord? Psalm 16:11 says that joy comes as a result of being in God's Presence. So if a person is going to greet people with infectious joy, he must spend time in the place where he can receive that joy — *in the Presence of the Lord.* You can see why the spiritual life of an usher or greeter is a very serious issue.

And how can a music leader effectively lead an entire congregation, home group, or Sunday school class into praise and worship if he or she never privately worships? To lead people in worship, one must be a worshiper.

The difference between a *professional singer* and a *real worshiper* is like night and day. A real worshiper lifts the people's hearts and souls higher, bringing them along with him or her into the Presence of God. A non-worshiper who leads praise and worship in a church is simply a song leader and nothing more. If you choose a non-worshiper to lead your worship service, the music may sound professional and the singers may sound great, but the worship will feel hollow because it lacks the Presence of God.

What happens in a public worship service to a great degree depends on the private spiritual life of the worship leader. His private devotional life will carry over into his public life. If he has no private worship life, the worship service in your church will be dissatisfying and unfulfilling.

As a pastor, this truth applies to me as well. I can teach Greek word studies, doctrine, illustrated sermons, and so on. But my ability to communicate *life* through those messages depends upon God's anointing on my life.

Without the anointing, my messages are simply empty words. But when the anointing comes, those same words become filled with power and life and have the ability to convict a sinner, reprove a believer, encourage one person, and give instruction to another. If the anointing is working through me, the Word I preach has the ability to touch and meet every single need in the congregation.

But for me to operate in that kind of anointing, I must have an active private spiritual life that is quickened by the Spirit of God. If I don't have a spiritual life, the congregation will sense it as I preach. Therefore, I can't wait until I get into the pulpit to prepare my spirit. I must remain in a constant state of preparation, waiting upon the Lord. This isn't an option for me. I must do this if I am to effectively do the job God gave me to do.

Once again, the private life of a leader is directly connected to the way he or she publicly serves. If his private life is full of God's Spirit, his ministry will likewise be filled with the Spirit and anointing of God. If his private life is void of any real spiritual substance, his public ministry will be void of that substance as well.

So before you lay hands on anyone, first delve into his personal life and find out what kind of private spiritual life this person has. Once you discover a positive answer to this question, you are in a position to move forward. But without this information, you're not prepared to make any kind of decision.

However, I've found that if I've applied the previous nine guidelines to the prospective candidate and he's scored well, I already know quite a bit about what kind of spiritual life he possesses. It takes a dimension of spiritual maturity to fulfill these other elements of one's life.

- If this person has desire;

- If this person is a good communicator;

- If this person has a home life that's in order;

- If this person is able to accept and flow with change;

- If this person gets along well with other people;

- If this person is receptive to correction;

- If this person has become essential to the operation of your church or organization;

- If this person came from another church with a good attitude and a favorable reputation;

- If this person is faithful with his tithes and offerings;

- Then you can be 99% sure that this person has a well-established spiritual life.

It takes a heart open to God to possess all the above-mentioned qualities in one's life. So if a candidate has done well on the first nine issues, I'm already fairly sure I understand his or her level of spirituality. The person couldn't fulfill the first nine guidelines without a close relationship with God and a solid private spiritual life.

OTHER QUESTIONS I ASK POTENTIAL LEADERS

It never hurts to delve into questions that pertain to a person's spiritual life in order to obtain the answers that you need. If you are that person's spiritual leader, you have every right to ask him penetrating questions about his relationship with God. If he resents your asking and thinks that this part of his life is off limits to you, don't even think about using that person in leadership. If you have no spiritual authority in his life, he doesn't have any business serving alongside you.

I ask each prospective leader questions that will give me clues regarding the kind of relationship he has with God. Certainly I can't discern everything about a person's spiritual life by interviewing him and asking questions. But the answers a potential leader gives me helps me obtain insights into his spiritual life. These insights are helpful as I determine whether or not this person has the spiritual constitution to lead people in spiritual matters.

So I ask the potential leader:

- Do you pray?

- How often do you pray?

- What do you pray about?

- Are there specific prayer burdens on your heart right now?

- Does God's Spirit speak to your heart?

- How do you know when God is speaking to you?

- How do you hear His voice?

- How much time do you spend reading your Bible?

- How often do you read your Bible?

- How do you study your Bible?

- Do you spend most of your time in the New or the Old Testament?

- When you read your Bible, does God speak to your heart?

- In what ways does God speak to your heart?

- Do you use other study helps as you read and study the Bible?

- Tell me about your worship life.

- Do you worship every day?

- How much time do you spend in worship?

- Do you pray in the Spirit?

- Approximately how much time do you spend praying in the Spirit during the course of a day?

- What happens inside you as you pray in the Spirit?

- Do you ever move in the gifts of the Holy Spirit?

- If so, which gifts?

- Is there anyone you're trying to win to Christ right now?

- If so, who is that person?

- In what ways are you trying to share Christ with that person?

- How much time do you spend in prayer with your family?

- Do you and your spouse read the Bible together?

- Do you and your spouse pray together?

- Is it difficult or easy for you to pray with your spouse?

- Do you ever discuss the Word of God with your children?

- How much time do you spend talking with your children about the Bible?

- Is there any specific thing in your life right now about which God is trying to deal with you?

- Can you identify that area of your life?

- What is your greatest spiritual challenge?

I don't intend to be intrusive by asking such questions, but how will I really know what's happening in that potential leader's life if I don't jump in and delve for these answers? I always begin such questions by making it plain that I'm only asking so I can obtain insights into his or her spiritual life. When they understand why I'm asking, I find very little resistance to my questions and interview.

I've found that pastors and ministry leaders often ask their potential leaders the *right* questions but not *enough* of the right questions. They ask about past employment, education, experience, family history, and future plans — and it's right to ask all these questions.

But when we're choosing people to serve as leadership in a church, ministry, or organization, we must not overlook this issue of the candidate's spiritual life. Questions related to a person's level of spiritual maturity are some of the highest-priority questions that can be addressed.

A FINAL WORD

The practical, down-to-earth guidelines I've given in this book are intended to reveal if a prospective leadership candidate is compatible enough with your own heart and standards to hold a leadership position in your church, ministry, business, or organization. My purpose has not been to put anyone through a grueling ordeal. Rather, I've endeavored to save both leader and follower from going *through* the grueling ordeal of becoming partners with someone whose standards don't fit well with their own.

When I myself have followed these ten guidelines, I've found that the process has nearly always exposed any problems I needed to know *before* I gave a person a place of leadership at my side. God may give you other ways to determine if a person is ready for leadership, but these guidelines have been helpful to our particular ministry.

In addition to all these guidelines, you must develop discernment from the Spirit of God about whom you should and should not use in your leadership team. So listen carefully to the voice of the Holy Spirit, and pay close attention to the scriptural principles I've written in this book. As you do, I believe you will make very few mistakes. By God's wisdom and grace, you'll select the leadership you need to take your ministry or organization to its highest level in God!

> You must develop discernment from the Spirit of God about whom you should and should not use in your leadership team.

QUESTIONS FOR PERSONAL GROWTH OR GROUP DISCUSSION

1. What happens when you try to minister to people without replenishing your own spiritual reserves?

2. What are some of the outward indications that a potential leader has a strong spiritual walk with God?

3. Describe the difference between 1) a professional singer or speaker, and 2) a true worshiper or preacher of the Word. What are the primary factors that create this difference?

4. What questions should you ask in order to determine the health of a prospective candidate's spiritual life?

5. What kind of responses to these questions would indicate that the candidate's spiritual walk has some serious deficiencies?

NOTES:

GREEK AND ENGLISH
NEW TESTAMENT STUDY HELPS
REFERENCE BOOK LIST

1. *How To Use New Testament Greek Study Aids* by Walter Jerry Clark (Loizeaux Brothers).

2. *Strong's Exhaustive Concordance of the Bible* by James H. Strong.

3. *The Interlinear Greek-English New Testament* by George Ricker Berry (Baker Book House).

4. *The Englishman's Greek Concordance of the New Testament* by George Wigram (Hendrickson).

5. *New Thayer's Greek-English Lexicon of the New Testament* by Joseph Thayer (Hendrickson).

6. *The Expanded Vine's Expository Dictionary of New Testament Words* by W. E. Vine (Bethany).

7. *New International Dictionary of New Testament Theology (DNTT)*; Colin Brown, editor (Zondervan).

8. *Theological Dictionary of the New Testament (TDNT)* by Geoffrey Bromiley; Gephard Kittle, editor (Eerdmans Publishing Co.).

9. *The New Analytical Greek Lexicon;* Wesley Perschbacher, editor (Hendrickson).

10. *The Linguistic Key to the Greek New Testament* by Fritz Rienecker and Cleon Rogers (Zondervan).

11. *Word Studies in the Greek New Testament* by Kenneth Wuest, 4 Volumes (Eerdmans).

12. *New Testament Words* by William Barclay (Westminster Press).

ABOUT THE AUTHOR

Rick Renner is a highly respected leader and teacher within the global Christian community. He is best described in a word — *excellence.* His passion for excellence in all areas, his love for God, and his calling as apostle and shepherd have made him a decidedly different Christian leader. These qualities have also made his ministry a distinctive organization, one that is an exceptional representation of excellence in all things.

Rick's organization has an international staff of approximately 200 people, and the lives touched by this ministry literally run into the millions worldwide. Internationally, Rick is recognized as a Bible teacher and conference speaker and is seen frequently on national TV network shows. He is a publisher and widely read author of many best-selling books and has also distributed hundreds of thousands of teaching audio and videotapes. He is President and Founder of *Rick Renner Ministries*, as well as a board member and counselor in various religious and commercial organizations.

Rick attended three different universities with an emphasis on Journalism and New Testament Greek and later earned a Doctor of Philosophy in Ministry. After ministering widely throughout the United States for many years, Rick answered God's call in 1991 to move his family to the former Soviet Union and plunge into the heart of its newly emerging Church. Rick has been featured multiple times in *Litsa*, a nationwide magazine published annually that features the 1,000 most influential people living in the Russian Federation. His weekly broadcast "Good News With Rick Renner" can be seen across the entire former USSR. Rick's past and present accomplishments include:

- Founder and President of the *International Good News Church*, better known as *Rick Renner Ministries.*

- Founder and owner of *Teach All Nations*, a book company that is taking God's Word to the nations of the world.

- Author of more than 30 books, including his internationally acclaimed *Sparkling Gems From the Greek* and several other bestsellers in the Christian market.

- Founder and Pastor of the *Moscow Good News Church*, one of the largest and fastest-growing Protestant churches in Moscow and throughout Russia.

- Founder and Pastor of the *Kiev Good News Church*, launched in 2007 in the heart of the capital city of Ukraine.

- Founder and President of the *Good News Association of Pastors and Churches* for Russia, Latvia, Ukraine, and Israel (through which he assists and strengthens more than 800 churches throughout the former Soviet Union and Israel).

- Founder and President of the *Moscow Good News Seminary*, a school that trains people who are called to be pastors and leaders in the emerging church of the former USSR.

- Founder and President of *Media Mir*, a commercial TV and print organization with distribution throughout Russia and the world.

- Founder and Chairman of *"It's Possible!"* (a humanitarian foundation that currently distributes vitamins monthly to thousands of pensioners in Moscow and is also involved in prison ministry, in orphanages, and in feeding the hungry).

- Founder and Chairman of the *Moscow Business Club*, an organization established to teach Christian business principles to entrepreneurs who live in Moscow and Russia.

- Founder and advisor to the *Riga Good News Church*, established in 1991 immediately following the collapse of the Soviet Union, which today numbers approximately 1,000 people.

Rick Renner Ministries has offices in the United States, Russia, Ukraine, Latvia, and England. Rick, Denise, and their family live in Moscow, Russia.

ABOUT OUR WORK
IN THE FORMER USSR

Since 1991 when God first called Rick and Denise Renner to the former Soviet Union, millions of lives have been touched by the various outreaches of *Rick Renner Ministries*. Nevertheless, the Renners' ever-increasing vision for this region of the world continues to expand across 11 time zones to reach 300 million precious lives for God's Kingdom.

The *Moscow Good News Church* was begun in September 2000 in the very heart of Moscow, right next to Red Square. Since that time, the church has grown to become one of the largest Protestant churches in Moscow and a strategic model for pastors throughout this region of the world to learn from and emulate. Today the outreaches of the *Moscow Good News Church* includes ministry to families, senior citizens, children, youth, and international church members, as well as a specialized ministry to businesspeople and an outreach to the poor and needy. In 2007, the Renners also launched the *Kiev Good News Church*, located in Kiev, Ukraine, as the next step in their ongoing vision to reach the former Soviet Union with the Gospel of Jesus Christ.

Part of the mission of *Rick Renner Ministries* is to come alongside pastors and ministers and take them to a higher level of excellence and professionalism in the ministry. Therefore, since 1991 when the walls of communism first collapsed, this ministry has been working in the former USSR to train and equip pastors, church leaders, and ministers, helping them attain the necessary skills and knowledge to fulfill the ministries that the Lord has given to them.

To this end, Rick Renner founded both a seminary and a ministerial association. The *Good News Seminary* is a school that operates as a part of the *Moscow Good News Church*. It specializes in training leaders to start new churches all over the former USSR and the nation of Israel. The *Good News Association of Pastors and Churches* is a church-planting and church-supporting organization that is now more than 800 pastors and churches strong!

Rick Renner Ministries also owns and operates the *Good News Television Network*, the first and one of the largest TV outreaches within the territory of the former USSR. Since its inception in 1992, this television network has become one of the strongest instruments available today for declaring the Word of God to the 15 nations of the former Soviet Union, reaching 110 million potential viewers every day with the Gospel of Jesus Christ.

In addition, Rick Renner also founded the *"It's Possible!"* humanitarian foundation, which is involved in various aspects of social evangelism in the city of Moscow. The *"It's Possible"* foundation uses innovative methods to reach different age groups of people whose needs have largely gone unmet by society. For example, every month in Moscow, the "Vitamin Club" program provides quality entertainment and distributes Christian literature and vitamins to approximately 3,000 elderly people — Russia's "forgotten generation."

If you would like to learn more about our work in the former Soviet Union, please visit our website at www.renner.org, or call 918-496-3213.

FOR FURTHER INFORMATION

For all book orders, please contact:

Teach All Nations

A book company anointed to take God's Word
to you and to the nations of the world.

A Division of
Rick Renner Ministries
P.O. Box 702040
Tulsa, OK 74170-2040
Phone: 877-281-8644
FAx: 918-496-3278
E-mail: tan@renner.org

*For prayer requests
or for further information about this ministry,
please write or call the Rick Renner Ministries office
nearest you (see following page).*

FREE PRODUCT CATALOG

To order a complete audio, video, and book catalog, please contact our office in Tulsa.

Rick Renner Ministries

www.renner.org

All USA Correspondence:
Rick Renner Ministries
P. O. Box 702040
Tulsa, OK 74170-2040
(918) 496-3213
Or 1-800-RICK-593
E-mail: renner@renner.org
Website: www.renner.org

Riga Office:
Rick Renner Ministries
Unijas 99
Riga, LV-1084, Latvia
(371) 780-2150
E-mail: info@goodnews.lv

Moscow Office:
Rick Renner Ministries
P. O. Box 53
Moscow, 109316, Russia
7 (095) 727-1470
E-mail: mirpress@umail.ru
Website: www.mgnc.org

Kiev Office:
Rick Renner Ministries
P. O. Box 146
Kiev, 01025, Ukraine
380 (44) 246-6552
E-mail: mirpress@rrm.kiev.ua

Oxford Office:
Rick Renner Ministries
Box 7, 266 Banbury Road
Oxford, OX2 7DL, England
44 (1865) 355509
E-mail: europe@renner.org

BOOKS BY RICK RENNER

BOOKS IN ENGLISH

Seducing Spirits and Doctrines of Demons

Living in the Combat Zone

Merchandising the Anointing

Dressed To Kill

Spiritual Weapons To Defeat the Enemy

Dream Thieves

The Point of No Return

The Dynamic Duo

If You Were God, Would You Choose You?

Ten Guidelines To Help You Achieve
    Your Long-Awaited Promotion!

It's Time for You To Fulfill Your Secret Dreams

Isn't It Time for You To Get Over It?

Sparkling Gems From the Greek Daily Devotional

Insights on Successful Leadership

365 Days of Power

BOOKS IN RUSSIAN

How To Test Spiritual Manifestations

Living in the Combat Zone

Merchandising the Anointing

Dressed To Kill

Spiritual Weapons To Defeat the Enemy

Dream Thieves

The Point of No Return

The Dynamic Duo

Hell Is a Real Place

Good News About Your New Life

What the Bible Says About Water Baptism

What the Bible Says About Tithes and Offerings

What the Bible Says About Healing

Signs of the Second Coming of Jesus Christ

It's Time for You To Fulfill Your Secret Dreams

Isn't It Time for You To Get Over It?

If You Were God, Would You Choose You?

Ten Guidelines To Help You Achieve Your
Long-Awaited Promotion!

The Death, Burial, and Resurrection of Jesus Christ

A Christian's Responsibility

If You Are Pursued by Failures

Insights on Successful Leadership

BOOKS IN GERMAN

Dream Thieves

The Point of No Return

Dressed To Kill

The Dynamic Duo

AUDIO SERIES BY RICK RENNER

Ministry and Servanthood

The Anointing

Miracles of Jesus Christ

The Person, Power, and Work
   of the Holy Spirit

Aggressive Worship

Spiritual Armor

Abraham, Father of Faith

Samuel, Spokesman of Almighty God

Prayers of the Apostle Paul

Seven Messages to the Seven Churches
   in the Book of Revelation

Supernatural Direction and Guidance

Six Important Messages to Leaders Today

Taking a Stand in Difficult Situations

Getting Rid of the Past

How To Respond if You've Received the Judas Kiss

Overthrowing Strongholds

Keys to Winning the Race of Faith

Healing the Mind and the Emotions
   of the Oppressed

Fulfilling God's Divine Destiny for Your Life

Seducing Spirits and Doctrines of Demons

Pulling Down Strongholds

How To Survive Difficult Situations

The Holy Spirit and You

How To Improve Your Relationship
   With Your Spouse, Part 1

How To Improve Your Relationship
   With Your Spouse, Part 2

How To Protect You and Your Family
   in the Last Days

If You're in a Trap, Here's How To Get Out

The Greatest Miracles of Jesus Christ

Wilt Thou Be Made Whole

The Will of God, Key to Success

Crossing the Bridge of Fear and Torment

Spiritual Weapons

How To Have Peace in Your Relationships

The Ministry of the Holy Spirit

Resisting the Enemy

Spiritual Warfare

It's Time To Get Over Bad Attitudes
   and Fix Your Stinking Thinking

VIDEOTAPES BY RICK RENNER

The Communion of the Holy Spirit

The Supernatural Assistance of the Holy Spirit

For We Wrestle Not Against Flesh and Blood

Biblical Approach to Spiritual Warfare

Wilt Thou Be Made Whole

Spiritual Error in the Church, Part 1

Spiritual Error in the Church, Part 2

Spiritual Error in the Church, Part 3

Qualifications of Leadership, Part 1

Qualifications of Leadership, Part 2

Submission and Authority, Part 1

Submission and Authority, Part 2

Pulling Down Mental Strongholds, Part 1

Pulling Down Mental Strongholds, Part 2

Seven Messages to the Seven Churches
— Overview of Seven Churches

Seven Messages to the Seven Churches — Rev. 2, John

Seven Messages to the Seven Churches — Ephesus

Seven Messages to the Seven Churches — Ephesus
and Smyrna

Seven Messages to the Seven Churches — Pergamus

The Help of the Holy Spirit, Part 1

The Help of the Holy Spirit, Part 2

The Help of the Holy Spirit, Part 3

Right Foundations, Part 1

Right Foundations, Part 2

New Supply of the Spirit

The Power of the Tithe

How To Survive in Difficult Situations, Part 1

How To Survive in Difficult Situations, Part 2

Abusive Situations in Work and Marriage, Part 1

Abusive Situations in Work and Marriage, Part 2

Abusive Situations in Work and Marriage, Part 3

Proper Attitude for Pursuing Your Purpose, Part 1

Proper Attitude for Pursuing Your Purpose, Part 2

How To Make Every Minute Count

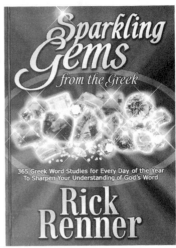

Insights on Successful Leadership

With every promotion comes greater responsibility and bigger challenges. Drawing on his own extensive experience as a leader, author Rick Renner has filled this little book with his own thought-provoking quotes on leadership, coupling each one with a pertinent and powerful scripture. Settle for nothing less than becoming the kind of leader God has called you to be!

$4.95 (Paperback)
ISBN: 0-9725454-3-3

Dynamic Duo

The Holy Spirit passionately yearns to fulfill His responsibility to the Father to help, teach, guide, and empower you. So if the cry of your heart is to walk as Jesus walked and to know the power of the Holy Spirit that the Bible speaks of, this is the book for you!

$10.99 (paperback)
ISBN: 0-88419-362-4

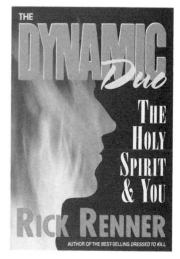

For more information, visit us online at: www.renner.org
Book Resellers: Contact **Teach All Nations** at 877-281-8644,
or e-mail tan@renner.org for quantity discounts.

Dressed To Kill

Rick provides vivid Greek word studies on every part of the spiritual armor God has given you, as well as helpful illustrations of the Roman armor used during New Testament times. You'll learn how to maintain your victorious position over Satan — every minute of the day!

$24.95 (Hardback)
ISBN: 978-0-9779459-0-0

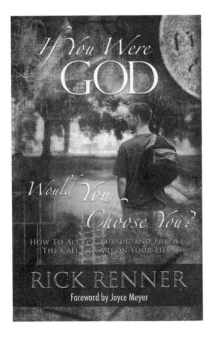

If You Were God, Would You Choose You?

What qualities does God look for when choosing His man or woman? This book contains a marvelous mixture of biblical teaching and life experience. There will be much to surprise and challenge you to say "YES" to all that God has for you!

$16.95 (Hardback)
ISBN: 978-0-9725454-9-5

For more information, visit us online at: www.renner.org
Book Resellers: Contact **Teach All Nations** at 877-281-8644,
or e-mail tan@renner.org for quantity discounts.

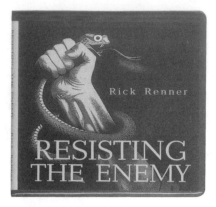
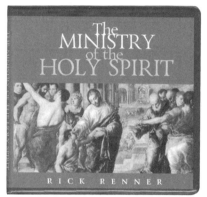
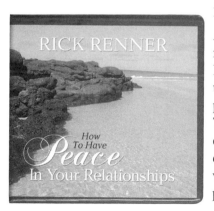

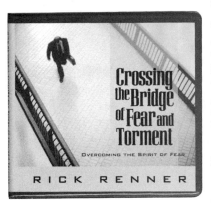

Crossing the Bridge
of Fear and Torment

Frustrations, fears, and torment come in all sizes and shapes. The enemy employs these tools in order to sabotage our life potential. Some fears and frustrations seem trivial, yet they leave lasting effects. Some come as a result of embarrassment over failures, leaving us alienated from friends, family, and even our God-appointed life purpose.

How do we get beyond our fears? How do we finally achieve victory over frustration and torment in our lives? Find out in this three-CD series as Rick delivers a message full of warmth and personal life experiences that will illuminate the Word of God and encourage you to move on.

$15.00 (3-CD series)

Spiritual Warfare

What does it take to "be strong in the Lord, and in the power of his might" (Ephesians 6:10)? How do you walk in the power of the Holy Spirit in your daily life? Rick seeks to answer these questions in his five-CD series "Spiritual Warfare." Gleaning from his extensive knowledge of New Testament Greek, Rick explains the various pieces of spiritual armor that God has given us to help us overcome every attack of the enemy.

$25.00 (5-CD series)

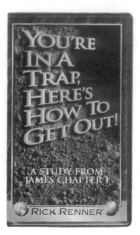

You're in a Trap, Here's How To Get Out

Do you feel as though there is no way out of your situation and you can't see the light at the end of the tunnel? Do you feel caged in by your adversary? Well, God has made a way of escape for you! In this six-tape series, you will learn the steps you must take to get out of any trap in which the enemy has ensnared you!

$30.00 (6-tape series)

Prayers of the Apostle Paul

Are you experiencing the riches of God's glory in your inner man? This powerful twelve-tape series explores how you can be delivered from the power of darkness and filled with all the fullness and knowledge of God. Learn how to draw from the Spirit of wisdom and revelation to become all God created you to be!

$48.00 (12-tape series)

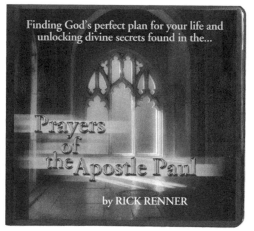

Wilt Thou Be Made Whole

Have you fallen victim to defeat, discouragement, or sickness and thus accepted less than God's best in your life? If so, Jesus is asking you the same question He asked a sick man in John 5: "Do you want to stay the way you are, or wilt thou be made whole?" This teaching will help you make the right choices so God can begin to heal you in every area of life — spirit, soul and body.

$20.00 (single videotape)

Laying the Right Foundations

Without a solid foundation under you, your life in God will not stand. Rick explains how to rely on God and His Word, not on any one individual, for the increase you need to build a strong foundation in your spiritual walk.

$20.00 (single videotape — part 1)
$20.00 (single videotape — part 2)

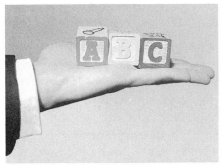

The Help of the Holy Spirit

In this three-part video series, you will gain new insight regarding the powerful ministry of the Holy Spirit in your life — to help you overcome your own spiritual infirmities.

Learn how the Holy Spirit has been sent to be your Helper and your own personal Tour Guide in a great adventure of faith. Let Him teach you how to disarm the lusts of the flesh and walk into a new life where victory is the rule and not the exception!

$20.00 (single videotape — part 1)
$20.00 (single videotape — part 2)
$20.00 (single videotape — part 3)

Do You Know What Time It Is?

You may have lost some opportunities in the past because you kept putting off what God told you to do. But it's never too late to stop wasting time! Denise Renner states: "These are crucial times we live in, and how we spend our time is a very serious matter. We must take the opportunity we have available right now to do what God has called us to do, because the clock is ticking, and time is passing us by." Let Denise inspire you to get back on track with God's purposes for your life as you pursue all that He has for you — every minute of every day!

$4.95 (128-page slimline book)
ISBN: 978-0-9725454-8-8

The Gift of Forgiveness

The act of forgiveness is one of the greatest yet most difficult commands that Jesus asks of us. Denise Renner draws both from the Word and from her own life experience to guide the reader from the depths of pain and despair to the ultimate act of love and emotional freedom through the act of forgiving others.

$3.50 (71-page slimline book)
ISBN: 0-9725454-4-1

Redeemed From Shame

In this book, Denise Renner demonstrates how the love of Jesus through the power of the Holy Spirit can set anyone free who has been emotionally crippled by shame in his or her life. Let the redeemed of the Lord say, "I am whole!" The message of *Redeemed From Shame* will change your life!

$3.50 (62-page slimline book)
ISBN: 0-9725454-5-X

For more information, visit us online at: www.renner.org
Book Resellers: Contact **Teach All Nations** at 877-281-8644,
or e-mail tan@renner.org for quantity discounts.

The Teaching Ministry of Denise Renner

Put Your Eye on the Prize
Forgiveness
Redeemed From Shame
Do You Know What Time It Is?

$20.00
(set of 4 messages on CD)

Songs About the Cross

Denise's newly remastered CD (formerly entitled, "The Gift of Forgiveness") is a collection of nine of the most beloved hymns about the Cross and the forgiveness that was purchased for us through the death of Jesus. These powerful hymns remind us of the great price Jesus paid for our redemption.

$15.00 — Music CD

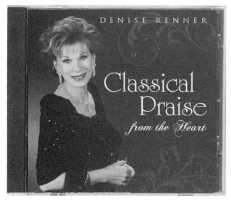

Classical Praise From the Heart

This is a magnificent production of classical songs that express a heart of praise unto the Lord. In this anointed CD by Denise Renner, you will hear the heart of an adoring child of God as Denise exalts the Lord through this wonderful collection of classical hymns and praise and worship songs.

$15.00 — Music CD

Collection Includes:

It Is Well With My Soul | Great Is Thy Faithfulness | Holy, Holy, Holy | I'd Rather Have Jesus | Hosanna | Love Medley | Thou Art Worthy | Jesus Medley | How Great Thou Art/ Amazing Grace (in Russian) | The Lord's Prayer (in Russian)

For more information, visit us online at: www.renner.org
Book Resellers: Contact **Teach All Nations** at 877-281-8644,
or e-mail tan@renner.org for quantity discounts.

STUDY NOTES

STUDY NOTES

STUDY NOTES

STUDY NOTES

STUDY NOTES

STUDY NOTES